FANTASTIC
MERCEDES-BENZ
AUTOMOBILES

TO MY MOTHER

FANTASTIC
MERCEDES-BENZ
AUTOMOBILES

The inimitable photographs of Peter Vann

with contributions by Clauspeter Becker, Uwe Brodbeck, Adriano Cimarosti, Rolf Kunkel, Dr. Harry Niemann and Antoine Prunet

Motorbooks International
Publishers & Wholesalers ®

Graphic layout and overall realization: Uli Praetor

Concept advisor: Claudine Renaux

Clothes, accessories and styling: Beatrice Dhenin, Paris

Translation of the English edition: Ruth Mason Herrlinger, Reutlingen

Proofreading: Dr. Wolfgang Herrlinger, Reutlingen

Typesetting: speedy typer desktop publishing gmbh, Reutlingen, Germany

Lithography: Repro Ludwig, Zell am See

Printing: Dr. Cantz'sche Druckerei, Ostfildern

Binding and sleeve: Buchbinderei Sigloch, Künzelsau

This edition first published in 1995 by Motorbooks International Publishers & Wholesalers, PO Box 2, 729 Prospect Avenue, Osceola, WI 54020 USA

Copyright 1994 Praetor & Rindlisbacher Verlagsgesellschaft mbH, Germany

Previously published in the German language by: Motorbuch Verlag of Stuttgart, Germany as Mythos Mercedes

Motorbooks International books are also available at discounts in bulk quantity for industrial or sales-promotional use.

For details write to Special Sales Manager at the Publisher's address.

Library of Congress Cataloging-in-Publication Data Available.

ISBN 0-7603-0015-1

On the front cover: 1930 Mercedes-Benz 500 SSK Roadster known as the "Count Trossi car" owned by Ralph Lauren.

On the back cover: Mercedes-Benz Special Roadster, 1936 (top left), Blitzen Benz, 1911 (top right),

Mercedes-Benz 300 SLR, 1955 (bottom left), Sauber-Mercedes C9, 1989 (bottom right)

Printed and bound in Germany

CONTENTS

**PETER VANN
A DIFFERENT VIEW
ON THINGS**

extravagance of the East. Compliant and well brought up, Peter agreed to complete a course of study in photography. With his diploma safely in his pocket, he took up a post as assistant to a fashion photographer. But he always felt himself attracted by another, more spectacular world far removed from the catwalks and the fashion studios: The theater, the lights, the music. Gripped by the urge to perform, he turned crooner. And the Peter Rindlisbacher that was became Peter Vann.

Switzerland soon proved too restricting as a stamping ground for the lively and cosmopolitan young performer, whose curiosity left him no peace. He traveled the length and breadth of Europe and discovered Paris. It was love at first sight. This inimitable city, which at last provided his romanesque temperament with the playground it had been longing for, was to become his future home.

WHEN PETER VANN TURNS his attention to cars, he does it in a different way to you or I. He studies them from a long way off. Not only because he uses a zoom lens, but because he has the unique talent of maintaining the necessary distance from his subject.

When he began to focus his activities on the automobile, Peter already had an unusual career behind him. Peter Rindlisbacher was born in Zurich in 1941. His father was German-speaking Swiss, his mother was of East Russian descent. This was a constellation which was to confront the young Peter from early childhood with an intriguing contrast: The straight-laced propriety of strict Protestantism interlaced with the exotic

Peter left Switzerland, the camera his mother had bought him stuffed into his baggage. He left vaudeville behind him too, picking up what he had put down by the wayside in his pursuit of fame and glamour: his photography. He started his career as a photographer working for the German magazine *Hobby*, where he worked in a team with Ursula.

It was purely by chance that one of his many reports brought him into contact with the subject of cars and motoring. His intuition told him that this special, very technical field was one in which he could make a unique mark of his own. The French journalist Jean-Paul Thévenet offered him regular employment with the magazine *"L'Automobile"*, paving the way for his debut on the stage of car photography.

At the beginning of the eighties, Peter Vann found himself beset by personal problems. Loyal friends helped him steer a course through this troubled period in his life, and he has rewarded them with sincere and undying affection. Through his prolific press work, an increasing number of contacts and connections opened up to him. It was not long before Peter was one of the most sought-after photographers working in the automobile scene.

His first book was published in 1983. It was followed by a further five or six volumes, all dedicated to vehicles past, present and future. Peter Vann has a unique way of paying homage to the automobile construed as a work of art or a sculpture. As a helpmate to designers, an advisor to collectors, a partner to design engineers as an illustrator whose work is esteemed by reporters everywhere, today Peter Vann is one of the most revered photographers of his generation.

In 1992, Peter Vann joined forces with one of his best and oldest friends, Uli Praetor, to produce his own magazine: *Auto Focus*. A publication which reflects something of the essential Peter Vann: Fascinating. Surprising. Offering a range of subject matter which places momentous events, encounters, friendship, loyalty and topicality firmly in the foreground. Hand in hand with the never-ending quest for beauty, elegance, refinement – all of which attributes Peter Vann captures with a precision bordering on the pedantic, of a kind shared by only a rare handful of his contemporaries. This new volume is dedicated to Mercedes-Benz. A company every bit in step with Peter Vann's taste.

Demanding and complex. Generous and strengthened by an eventful past. Working with a handful of revered authors, Peter Vann took up the search for models which most aptly reflected the long and rich tradition of their manufacturer. In his travels in search of material, his path crossed with those of many of those illustrious personalities whose stories play such a decisive role in the telling of this unique tale. With that of Juan Manuel Fangio, for example, in which we discover the land of his childhood and the car he drove to some of his spectacular successes. A fascinating mixture of places and epochs.

More than any of his preceding works, this book bears witness to the meticulous care Peter Vann vests in every one of his pictures. His search for the right motifs, the choice of perspective, the lighting. Untiring, Peter will spend days searching for the right background – which is always majestic, whether taken from nature or from momentous works of architecture. Fire, ice, aluminium: Games with materials and colors, with shading and matchless tone-in-tone effects.

Restless and yet self-confident, concentrated and yet imaginative, Peter Vann puts his disarming obstinacy to the test again and again. The perfectionist will move heaven and earth to obtain just the right light conditions. Even if it means spraying several hundred meters of asphalt with water or leveling a whole quarry to obtain that special effect. Out on location, Peter Vann barks out incomprehensible instructions with all the high-strung temperament of the artist at work. But back home in his apartment in the Le Marais quarter of Paris, he winds down, is at peace with himself. Surrounded by his children, his memories, his Art-deco bric-a-brac, his operas. Somewhere between Wagner and Bellini.

Serge Bellu

THE ONE AND ONLY

THE SINGLE MOST IMPORTANT WORD IN JUAN MANUEL FANGIO'S VOCABULARY: FRIENDS.
IT WAS THEY WHO MADE IT ALL POSSIBLE – FROM HIS RISE AS A BOY FROM THE PAMPAS TO THE FULFILLED
EXISTENCE OF A DISTINGUISHED ELDERLY GENTLEMAN

A visit to Argentina in November 1993

AT LAST THE NEWS we had hardly dared hope for from Argentina. Fangio's state of health had improved to a degree that he would be able to receive us. Instead of the secretary, the reins of organization would now be placed in the hands of Fangio's lady friend who was a better judge of what the now frail Fangio would be able to cope with. He looked forward to our visit... a letter unmistakably of the wonderful old school where the word etiquette still counted for something.

We had the Director of the Mercedes Museum in Stuttgart, Max von Pein, to thank for arranging this once-in-a-lifetime visit. On familiar terms with Fangio for decades, he had also made a major contribution to the founding of the Fangio Museum in Argentina. Max von Pein was intimate with all the friends and relatives we were to meet, and on the strength of his recommendation we were met with open arms by this big and warm-hearted South American family.

Fangio never married, but had always been what they used to call a ladies' man. It came as no real surprise that, at the age of 82, his companion should be an attractive lady of high standing in Argentina with an aristocratic background. She invited us to a first dinner party in her Buenos Aires penthouse near the Recoleta, the stamping ground of the well-to-do.

Fangio arrives at on the dot of ten – the evening meal is taken late in Argentina. We had prepared ourselves psychologically to encounter someone not in the best of health, but on meeting Fangio face to face we suddenly seemed to forget about the story we had come here to write. We were moved at the thought of the honor done us by this frail old gentleman simply by his appearance. It suddenly seemed inconceivable that we should fly with him the next day to Mar del Plata, visit the ranch. Fangio appeared so incredibly weak, so fragile. Even Lili was unable to look at him without tears in her eyes.

His last setback happened in the autumn of 1993 in Germany, when he was taken to a Stuttgart clinic suffering from a bout of enteritis on top of kidney trouble. His friends, including Hans Herrmann and Max von Pein, immediately gathered around him. Despite being assured that a kidney transplant was still on the cards even at his advanced age, Fangio refused any such treatment outright. His grounds were not expressed in so many words, but there are reasons to assume that he has moral qualms about the unnatural use of human spare parts. However that may be, there was no moving him on that front, and transplantation as an option was strictly rejected.

Fangio encourages us to talk about Europe, pays attention, missing nothing. He speaks in Spanish quietly, with a highish-pitched sing-song voice. He never set any store by learning English, and his German is about as extensive as Stirling Moss's: "Ja, Herr Neubauer."

*Fangio born in 1911
and the Mercedes 300 SLR
from 1954. The car was taken
out the automobile museum
of Balcarce which is the
champion's native town*

We carefully broach the subject of Argentina's beauty beyond Buenos Aires, and it seems we will be traveling alone. Lili anxiously reads Fangio's eyes, and seeing something there which escapes the rest of us, seems pleased. Fangio explains that he would like to rest the next day, we should fly out to Mar del Plata where we would be met by his friends and make ourselves familiar with the area, find the best photo locations. He would follow the next day on the early flight together with Lili. Rely on me, he said, I will come, it is something I want to do.

Balcarce lies around one hour's drive from Mar del Plata, past pampa pure, devoid of people or buildings but graced by plenty of attractive cattle. Balcarce is the potato capital of the country, and in its heyday supplied 70 per cent of the entire country's requirement. We differentiate between the various sorts – Rosa Blanca, Sierra Larga, Nuero Nueve and Spunta, while guests from Europe prefer the large, longish Kenebek.

The small town of Balcarce and the Juan Manuel Fangio legend are inextricably bound up with each other. The interwoven fates of the two are something difficult to grasp from the European perspective and in the present day and age. It is hard to imagine what an isolated and gloomy existence it must have been here, and how hard life must have been for the ten-year-old at the beginning of the twenties, chased out of bed at four in

the morning to pore over his books before clocking in as apprentice at the local foundry. At twelve he moved on to a mechanical engineering workshop. The machines he had to work on and the methods used to coax them into life defy imagination: "The best tool we had for machining a piston was a handily-shaped stone".

He learned the art of driving while still in his early teens by delivering cars from the workshop, on unmetalled roads of course, under conditions which in the rainy season ranged between slippery slime and deep mud. Fangio claims that the morass teaches just about everything you need to know about driving: How to approach with plenty of momentum, to develop the right degree of intuition to cope with unforeseen situations, and most importantly of all, not to brake whatever happens.

The most important word which crops up as Fangio talks about those early experiences: Friends. It was they who made everything possible. For example, the uncertain financial adventure of his first races which were made possible by the loan of a taxi from a friend of Fangio's father. Each new project was met with an even greater show of support, to the extent of public collections in the streets of Balcarce. The next ingenious idea was to hold a lottery. The prize: The car which Fangio would drive in the race as soon as he had scraped enough cash together from the sale of lottery tickets. The only sponsor mentioned on the car was the name of

the town: The man from Balcarce is on his way.

Needless to say, the car racing madness which was running at fever pitch in Argentina at the time helped give the whole money-raising campaign the necessary impetus. When a local lad had drive enough to pitch his skill against the bigwigs from the town it was enough to turn him into something of a local hero here in the capital of potato country. His provincial origins were also enough to secure the sympathy of more neutral observers, and his cause was adopted by the towns of Mar del Plata and Rosario. Still today, Rosario continues to consider Fangio as its own progeny, donating the most splendid trophies, devising the most touching tributes.

The long road races he contested, often 5,000 kilometers and more, in generously lightened American limousines, made the now around thirty-year-old lad from Balcarce a household name in Argentina by 1942. It was then that the repercussions of World War II, which had previously left neutral Argentina unaffected, became so great as to put a complete stop to motor racing until the end of the war. Fangio was then 34 and unknown in the world of international motor racing. He had never seen Europe, and Europe had never heard of him.

The President of the Fangio Foundation goes by the name of Luis Barragán. The Foundation takes care of the museum, the ranch, the racetrack. Its members are all members of Balcarce's population, and naturally enough all Fangio's friends, generally the sons of the men Fangio grew up with, who repaired cars with him, helped him scrape together money, played football with him (Fangio is reputed to have played a mean right half-back in his youth). All people of a practical leaning, the Foundation members represent just about every key function in the town – chemist, manufacturer, agricultural engineer, farmer, architect, department store owner, boss of the local power plant. Their names reflect a potted history of immigration into Argentina, ranging over the entire spectrum from Basques to Catalans, Castilians to Greeks, Italians, Arabs. And every one is known familiarly by a nickname. One of the peculiarities about life in Argentina is that practically no-one goes by their actual name. Ali Muso, who stored 400 Fangio cups in his cellar before the museum was built, is known as "Camel", or "El Turco". "Camel" he can live with, but his other nickname he accepts only with grudging resignation considering that the only connection his Syrian fathers ever had with the Turkish was to have their throats cut by them.

The sense of pride these men feel in Fangio is something which comes straight from the heart. They would move heaven and earth or submit to all kinds of torture for their hero. But at the same time there is no overlooking the benefits they derive from their foundation membership. According to the statute, the membership must number exactly twelve, and when they come together formally then with all the ceremony of an ancient council. Meetings are generally followed by the inevitable get-together round a laden supper table. The Donna Elviras left at home know what it means when there is a "meeting on".

The museum is accommodated in a splendid house built during the wealthy end of the last century on Balcarce's main square. The interior architecture with its ramps is reminiscent of the Mercedes Museum in Stuttgart.

Fangio's brother, Ruben, known as Toto.
It was here in his workshop that the legend was born

gart, and indeed is the work of the same architect. The collection of exhibits has nothing of the run-of-the-mill local museum about it: This is a big automobile exhibition with Fangio as its focus. Fangio memorabilia intermingles with photos, certificates, trophies and of course cars, including the 1955 Mercedes Silver Arrow.

I am particularly taken with the two superb „Balcarce" Chevrolet models built in 1939 and 1940. Bearing the number 38, Fangio drove in the Argentinean Grand Prix, a road event covering over ten thousand kilometers. Once again it was the town of Balcace which had rallied round to scrape together enough cash to buy him a Ford. They fell short of their target and only managed a Chevy – second choice because as everyone knew, the '39 Chevy had such an appetite for oil. So they set about testing out every Chevy they could lay hands on among friends and acquaintances, and in the end it was potato farmer Arturo Vuotto who won the day: He was given the privilege of donating his engine because it used the least oil.

First leg: A damaged connecting rod, hasty repairs en route and position 119 in Santa Fé. The oil loss was so tremendous that Fangio went to the length of drilling a hole in the instrument panel and feeding a pipe through from the oil tank to within reaching distance of the co-pilot's mouth. As many oil canisters as they could carry were loaded on board and long-suffering Héctor Tieri (who had pleaded in favor of Ford and only Ford from the start) had the unenviable task of blowing fresh supplies forward, while the inside of the car filled with the vapors of the rapidly escaping used oil. But what turned out to be an even greater problem was the mud and sludge on the roads, causing so much wheel slip that the clutch eventually burned out. They jacked up the Chevy, took off all the wheels, opened her up, scraped out the wheel houses – at which stage Fangio managed to lose his shoes irretrievably in the mud. The intrepid barefoot pilot and his mate arrived 108th in Paraná. After coming a considerably more hopeful 18th in Concordia, they could get no further and interrupted the race to load the cars onto the train to Cordoba. Despite repairs to the rear crankshaft bearing, they were unable to stop either water coming in or oil escaping. Fangio, inventive as ever, fashioned a seal from the brass-reinforced rim of an old felt hat which held up long enough to get them to Santiago del Estero in eighth position. This made them the first Chevrolet in the race and got them a mention on the national radio. After coming third in Jujuy, where they were actually presented with two free new tires to help them on their way in style, it was plain sailing all the way: Second position in Catamarca – coinciding with Fangio's appointment as Chevrolet works pilot – and then on to tackle the Fords with a first position in Nonoquasta and San Juan. He actually finished only fifth after another slight accident and a further bout of repairs on the Chevy, but he had made his indelible stamp on the annals of motor racing history in Argentina, and in the hearts of the population of Balcarce. Famous, he returned to a town rocked with adulation. Today, that memorable vehicle is there in the museum for all to see, and even touch. The funniest thing about it are the seats, perched up on top of the tank – behind them more tank, the whole interior is nothing but tank. The whole of the luggage compartment too. The 3.5 liter six-cylinder Chevy offered up 90 horsepower at 3300 revs, and reached a top speed of 145 kph. Next to this venerable exhibit is the donation list showing all the townsfolks' contributions, ranging from 0.50 to 500 pesos.

And then there are the trophies. The cup presented by the Cuban dictator Battista, over a yard high. But the most magnificent are the Italian ones, sculptured figures depicting goddesses of victory, naked of course, with heaving bosoms undulously proclaiming the glory of supremacy in the chase. Motor racing takes on a deeper meaning as you gaze in awe and fascination.

A list of honorary citizenships as long as your arm, Fangio taking pride of place on the 30 peso postage stamp, pictures hobnobbing with presidents and the likes of Frank Sinatra or Niki Lauda. Trophies shaped like Roman war chariots and Greek goddesses, the 1923 Hudson and the special car designed by his brother Toto in 1947 in which Fangio caused a sensation in Rosario. Perhaps the most important car from those early days, it went by the name of Negrita, the little negro. But what do we mean by early days exactly? Fangio had already turned 36 and was still a stranger to Europe.

We are accompanied by Luis Barragán, President of the Fangio Foundation who everybody just calls "Negro". Is it really true that all Argentineans are only addressed by nicknames, I want to know from Luis, or rather El Negro, and how about Fangio? Do people really all call him El Chueco?

After a good three minutes' reflection – even the locals are affected by the heat, after all - Luis launches on a lengthy explanation: The names we are christened with are there to form relationships with those we honor particularly - with saints, relatives or anyone else. In Fangio's case there was practically no alternative. If a boy is born on June 24th, St. John's day, there is only one thing for it: to call him Juan. And if that boy's father, as in the case of Don Loreto, had been an ardent monarchist in his former homeland, there no was no doubt in anyone's mind that he must

honor Vittorio Emmanuele II somehow too – hence Manuel. But when after thirteen or fourteen years it turns out on the football pitch that neither John the Baptist nor His Majesty the King of Italy can prevent the young Argentine boy from developing bow legs, so be it: The popular appendage from then on simply has to be Chueco, or old bow legs to us.

All very well, I object, but how can it be that a man who has been honored with just about every accolade and is a dignified and revered hero of the people has to be reminded at every turn about the lack of linearity in his legs. I cannot help but express my admiration for the charm demonstrated by the Biographer Molter, who described Fangio walking up to receive a prize from Prince Ranier „with the rocking gait of cavalryman".

The President, we should say El Negro, sitting at the edge of the yellow bushes, becomes more insistent: If someone is called by a name referring either to a physical characteristic or his place of origin, this is not meant as anything derogatory. He, Luis Barragán, reminds people of a negro because of his healthy color and his muscular build, and if people care to call him that, it does not imply condescension at all, but on the contrary, affection.

The next stage of our visit takes us to the Fangio Foundation ranch. It is not a real ranch as we generally understand the word, but a beautiful piece of land accommodating farmhouses and bungalows, a swimming pool and tennis court. It is a haven in which to honor Fangio, in which the grand master himself can relax in the company of the closest of the clan, "the Foundation". The special charm of this oasis lies in its enormous trees, between which are strewn buildings, and in whose branches the permanently cooling breeze has the most charming stories to whisper. I cannot remember any other place in which falling asleep and waking up are such a delicious experience.

The biggest building on the ranch is a plain, empty hall like a post-modern church or an ancient Polynesian place of worship.

"What goes on here?", I asked attentively.

"This is where we come together to eat", said Luis. "When we get down to some serious eating, this is where we do it."

"Are special types of food served here?", I asked, fascinated by the cult-like aspect of the austere building.

"Meat". El Negro's reply was uttered with a benevolent, almost pious air. "We eat a lot of meat in here".

He went on to explain that on special occasions or celebrations for the whole clan, or when – for whatever reason – enough friends had been brought together to surround the enormous board accommodated in the hall, hour upon hour would be spent consuming inordinate quantities of sausages and sirloins, washed down by liter upon liter of beer and wine: something which defies the imagination of the uninitiated European.

We partook of a modest snack that evening, perhaps a kilo of sausages and steak each or so, and discussed the photographic session on the following day. Peter Vann was keen to disperse various trophies and cups around the area and shoot some snaps of Fangio with them (the word "snap" slips out as a sort of unintentional expression of my frustration at the generally roundabout way in which all photographers go to work). We also discussed our plans to take a car from the museum for some open-air shots: The 300 SL Roadster.

Which brings us round to the Mercedes era. Seven as yet uncharted years lie between the post-war limbo and Fangio's glorious victories. An attempt to cover some ground:

Although it had remained neutral during the war (up until a token declaration of war six weeks before the German capitulation), Argentina suffered from the same wartime raw material shortages as every other country. Petrol was at a premium, giving rise to a four-year halt on all motor racing in the country. When it started – in 1947 – Fangio was 36 years of age and an unknown entity in Europe.

In Argentina, this period saw the beginning of the Perón dictatorship. Since "Evita", the story is old hat to everyone: Perón with his hair dripping with Brillantine, his wife Eva, beautiful, pale and of course blonde, champion of the poverty-stricken, who sadly suffered from lung trouble and so found herself forced to sing "Don't cry for me, Argentina". And in the middle of all this high drama, we imagine Fangio.

In retrospect, the Perón era can be seen as a giant Argentine social reshuffle in various directions. Corrupt certainly, but with an almost pioneering quality when we compare it to the South American regimes which were to follow it. Essential elements of the regime were Perón's gushy manner, Evita's charm and the populist ties of national self-esteem.

It is only against this background that we are able to conceive how, in years of such hardship, it was possible for international car races to be contested, European racing drivers invited to take part and the National Automobile Club to be in a position to equip an Argentinean racing team and send it off to Europe. While all this was going on, Fangio was still little more than the shrewd mechanic from the potato town, but he was ready to stand in as a possible driver "for Argentina" – and seized the chance with both hands. Needless to say, the Dictator later turned the situation to account as soon as Fangio had become the hero of the nation. When Peronism ended in 1955, Fangio was subjected to a short-lived victimization campaign, but fundamentally he was and remained an untouchable within the State of Argentina. Perhaps another way to put it would be like this:

Without the nationalistic muscle-flexing of the Perón regime, Fangio would never have been given the opportunity to make it to Europe. Otherwise Fangio had no truck with politics, excepting once when he was on the receiving end of political violence (kidnapping in Cuba - more about that later), from which he emerged victorious, a role model. This is something which doubtless affords him great satisfaction to think back on: He always considered the obligation to be a model to others something which would brook no compromise, and this belief fires a tremendous discipline in the man still today.

The vehicles procured by the Automobile Club of Argentina for the national racing team were a Simca-Gordini and three four-cylinder Maseratis. Generous though this may seem, conditions for the Argentinean team were worlds apart from those of today's motor racing heroes. Fangio generally used to spend the night before the race sleeping in the transporter. Things began to get off the ground for him in 1949 when he won four races in succession with Maserati against medium-caliber – not yet the very best – competitors (San Remo and three French races). Reflecting the national enthusiasm, two Argentinean radio reporters followed the team to Europe. They succeeded in stirring up a veritable whirlwind of frenzied enthusiasm back home, and after the fourth victory, the radio was already broadcasting the Fangio Tango. This produced an irresistible

degree of pressure for the shooting star to be put at the wheel of a more competitive vehicle in the run up to Monza. A Ferrari 166 was procured on the strength of a promise in the form of an unsecured IOU, and when Fangio lived up to every expectation in the big race he was assured his first hero's welcome in Buenos Aires, led naturally enough by General Perón.

By 1950, Fangio was already 39, but now a works driver for the first time in his life. The legendary "Three Fs" Alfa Romeo team – Farina, Fagioli and Fangio – entered the world's first official Formula One Driver's Championship. Six races counted towards the final result, and the supercharged Alfettas swept the board every time. But as Fangio was forced to retire three times with technical trouble, winning every other race was still not quite enough to secure him overall victory: Farina took the title, Fangio came a close second.

The 1951 season was considerably more exciting, as a major strategic decision by Enzo Ferrari wrought a decisive change in the face of Formula One racing: He decided to back the 4.5 liter aspirated engine (instead of the 1.5 liter supercharger), and order the construction of the famous Lampredi-V12. Once everything was in place, Ferrari actually won its first World Championship race, but then this new Ferrari 375 was not reliable enough to stop Fangio, now clearly number one on the Alfa team. At forty, he became World Champion for the first time. Campeón del mundo! Argentina could hardly contain itself.

Motor racing in those days meant variety, with much less of the Formula One World Championship fixation which marks the sport nowadays. Fangio felt at home driving for Alfa and was keen to wait for the introduction of their new sports car. Another factor was that the South

*"Fangiodrom" near Balcarce:
Museum piece 300 SLR, President of
the Foundation Luis Barragán,
whose life work is to channel all the
warmth of affection felt for the
one-time Champion into the
creation of a total art work
to serve as a worthy memorial for
generations to come*

American season was highly important to him (in a Ferrari belonging to the Automobile club). Beyond that, he would wait and see what became of the Grand Prix events. There was the adventure with the legendary British development, the 16-cylinder BRM, Maserati would be honored if requirement arose – but in the meantime came June 8, 1952.

Fangio had just completed a tough trip from Northern Ireland to Milan, drove through the night, arrived in Monza at 2.00 p.m., only to be informed that the organisers would allow him to line up despite not having been at the training session. Nothing daunted, he betook himself to the grid at 2.30 p.m. in a Maserati, overtook six cars in the first lap, had a slight skirmish in the Lesmo bend, failed to react quickly enough, rolled over and was flung free of the car.

"I didn't feel anything. There was no time to be aware of fear or pain. The pain caught up with me later in hospital. When I came round, I began to remember things which had led up to the accident - and how thin the line was between life and death!"

Fangio survived three months in plaster to emerge a new man, apart from a stiff neck which left him with the posture which came to be known as one of his trademarks. The Champion has (literally) not looked back over his shoulder since.

So 1952 was a year best forgotten, 1953 also something of a disappointment. Ferrari with Alberto Ascari was still the dominating force in the World Championships, Fangio had to be satisfied with Maserati (not forgetting the Monza victory) and BRM. However, the end of the season saw his spectacular victory on Lancia D24 in the Carrera Panamericana against the superior might of the Ferraris.

The two-liter World Championship formula now came to an end, and 1954 marked the beginning of new regulations. Mercedes had been working up to this moment and a return to Formula One racing for two years. In his memoirs, the legendary Head of Racing at Mercedes, Alfred Neubauer, recalls a conversion with Fangio in 1953, in whichever language it may have taken place:

How about it this time, Señor? Works driver for Mercedes-Benz next year perhaps?

Herr Neubauer, was Fangio's reply, I am not a guinea pig. Who can guarantee that your new car won't be a flop?

Fangio cannot remember being quite so reticent. He had been owner of a Mercedes dealership in Buenos Aires since 1951, and the mechanic in him had a soft spot for the Stuttgart marque. He used to hold long pep talks about the benefits of the 170 diesel engine before the W196 had even made it to the drawing board. Reliability is and always was one of the most important virtues in Fangio's book, and he demanded it both of people and of machines. In many respects he was the typical old-fashioned Mercedes diesel customer. And everyone involved took for granted that the best marque in the world would approach the best driver in the world for its Grand Prix comeback. That there should be a token display of coyness, a little light foreplay, was something the portly Neubauer owed to his already mythical reputation and Fangio to his Argentine Italian roots and his pride in the broadest sense. It is important to remember that he was already well into maturity when his racing career really took off the ground.

Our visit had excited quite a stir in Balcarce. Since Fangio's state of health had taken such a dramatic turn for the worse in the Summer of '93, he had not been back to visit his home town. His long absence had unsettled the Clan, which kept itself informed every day of the latest developments from Buenos Aires.

The organization functions smoothly and precisely in the background, powered by an enormous underlying affection for the man. Tearjerking apart, it is the simple truth that there are friends and relatives among these warm-hearted people whose most fervent wish is that Fangio should see their children once again and to whom this is of insurmountable importance.

Jobs are distributed with detailed precision to involve as many "disciples" as possible. It starts with positioning the gangway at the Mar del Plata airstrip, and continues with the convoy who will flank his car on the drive to Balcarce, and especially the Chauffeur. Ali Muso, also known as "Turco", also known as "Camel", will have the honor. Peter Vann had chosen the 1955 300 SL Roadster which had been taken from the Museum as his first photographic motif. Our friends took the car to the racetrack. In the meantime, brother Toto joined us. The gathering of the clan was under way.

And at long last: Fangio arrives with Lili. Quarter of an hour spent in a moving scene of greeting, then photos. We discover that Fangio is no longer able to climb into the narrow cockpit. Not to worry, I reassure him, forget the cockpit shot, we will try something quite different. Fangio flares up in an instant: No, we are going to do this photo, all I need is a bit of help. Max von Pein and I do the honors. A narrow squeeze of a car with a high side sill, and Fangio is just a featherweight.

1954 went smoothly, everything according to plan. Until Mercedes had its Grand Prix car ready, Fangio won with Maserati, and when Mercedes finally pulled the drapes of its creation, Fangio won with Mercedes.

The long-awaited and much publicized return of the Silver Arrow took place on July 4, 1954, at the French Grand Prix in Reims. The date coincided with the final of the football World Cup in Bern. Germany beat Hungary and had found its place in the world again.

It was really the impact of a double victory on its very first appearance which made the post-war version of the Silver Arrow legend such a sensation. Fundamentally, no-one should have been too surprised at the superiority of the W196. After all, Stuttgart had used all those bright sparks who had helped put life into the pre-war racing car, they had been working for two years on a new definition of the state of the art and on its consistent application in the current 2.5 liter formula.

Towards the end of the 1954 season, Fangio enjoyed such an invincible position in the World Championship (his second), and stood out as such a monumental personality against the rest of the field that the time seemed somehow ripe for a change of scenario. With brand new regulations, there was not much that could be done from the technical point of view. What the racing world was waiting for was the arrival of a new hero.

He was not long in coming.

Stirling Crauford Moss, born in 1929, a Virgo. This distinctively British personality found a matching British car in every motor racing class except Formula One, where he had no alternative but to look for foreign assistance – although the Golden Age of English Formula One racing prowess was just around the corner (Vanwall from 1956 onwards, followed by Cooper, BRM, Lotus, Aston Martin, Brabham and so on through to McLaren). Moss splashed out what would now be the equivalent of around 25,000 pounds on his own Formula One Maserati, had it sprayed Racing Green and used it to see off the older generation of pre-war drivers still pounding the circuits of Europe. In 1955 he was already negotiating with Ferrari, but allowed himself to be wooed by Stuttgart in the end.

The 1955 Mercedes line-up: Fangio, Karl Kling, Hans Herrmann, Stirling Moss.

The main opposition it faced was from Ferrari (Farina, Hawthorn, Gonzalez, Maglioli, Trintignant), Lancia (Ascari, Villoresi, Castellotti), Maserati (Behra, Musso) and Gordini (Schell).

The very first race meeting which took place with this constellation was the Argentine Grand Prix. All the statistics show this to have been the most hotly contested Formula One race ever to have taken place right up to the present day. The distance covered was almost double that of to-day's Grand Prix events, and it was an act of mercy on the part of the organizers that this particular race was limited to three hours. Temperatures in the nineties must sound comparatively cool to someone who has had to ride out those three hours on what was literally a hot seat - a tunnel which the driver had to straddle to operate the gas and clutch pedals, which were some 60 cm apart.

Moss, behind Fangio in second position, came to a standstill as he drove out of a curve, mouthed something that looked like "vaporizing" and threw himself onto the grass. He was soon bundled into a Red Cross Ambulance, but by the time they reached the pits he was already knocking to be let out. By this time everyone had driven as long as they could stand. Hans Herrmann had already dropped out, and his car had been taken over

by Kling, whose own chariot had been damaged at the beginning of the race. When Kling arrived in the pit, exhausted, an unperturbed Moss got in and drove the race to its bitter end, coming in fourth.

Prior to this, the Ferraris initially driven by Gonzales and Farina had each gotten through three drivers to come in second and third. But in pride of place, lonely at the front of the field, sat Fangio – by no means the youngest in the field. He thought his car must have caught fire, but what he could feel was just the hot air from the engine flowing over his neck and shoulders: "The track was shimmering so much that it looked like a reflection of the sky. To stop myself from going crazy, I imagined I was someone who had lost their tracks in the snow, and that I would freeze to death unless I trudged onwards. I painted myself that picture every time I got to the straight, and at the same time I leant forward in my seat to try and keep the burns on my legs off the scalding hot grid."

Fangio, single-handed, won the Grand Prix with second degree burns on both legs.

Moss was just 25, Fangio 43. They continued to compete against each other for a further three years, but only in 1955 in the intimacy of the same team. The division of roles between them went unspoken, Moss following undaunted in the tracks of the master. So closely at times that he got sick from the exhaust fumes (Monaco), had sand from the dunes thrown up inside his engine (Zandvoort), or fell foul of flying stones (Monza). An exasperated Neubauer issued warnings to Moss on each of these occasions. But he had achieved what he wanted: "I learned more following Fangio's line than in all the previous years put together." It is perhaps just as well to call to mind again that the period we are talking about was the heyday of the powerslide: Engine performance had achieved a sufficient height (290 bp) and sufficient control (without supercharger), and the tires were dreadful enough to provide that tidy four-wheel drift which later got lost among the slicks and the state-of-the-art chassis.

Stirling Moss recalls: "Sometimes when I was following close behind him he used to let the car skid sideways into a narrow bend so I could see his face. I used to grimace at him, and he would grin back, then we would dash off like a couple of puppies."

The racing drama that year played away from the Formula One stage, on that blackest of days in motor racing history, June 11, 1955, in Le Mans.

Just in front of the pit, where the crowd of spectators was at its most tightly packed, Levegh in a works Mercedes was unable to swerve in time to avoid a slower Austin Healey with Macklin at the wheel. The Mercedes mounted the other car, flew into the air and smashed into the crowd where it burst into flames. The impact of the engine alone must have killed dozens. The total number of deaths was a horrendous 83, and the accident marked the most devastating motor racing catastrophe of all times.

Even following years of painstaking investigation, the question of guilt was never finally settled. Mike Hawthorn (Jaguar) was considered to blame by many: It was his late, abrupt decision to take a pitstop and sudden braking maneuver that forced the Healey out of its track and into the path of the fast approaching Levegh Mercedes. Footage shot by an amateur cameraman, which was only professionally evaluated during the seventies, would seem to establish Hawthorn's innocence. Leaving that aside: Just behind Levegh was the fastest Mercedes just about ready to lap the cars in front, and in it sat Fangio.

Fangio recalls: "It was pure chance, it was fate, the will of God, call it what you will. I drove straight through the middle of the crash scene without touching anything or anyone. Directly afterwards I began to tremble like a leaf: I had been just waiting for the impact and had been holding onto the steering wheel for dear life. Instead, a hole in the chaos had opened up and I had slipped through it."

This is the reconstruction of events which Fangio stands by still today. Since that day there

Fangio pilots the Mercedes W196 in the British Grand Prix of 1955. An icon of the sports shirt generation, as well as a magnificent example of the photographic skills of Louis Klemantaski, the most significant motor racing photographer of the day

have been innumerable Fangio statements superimposed in different versions and the original Fangio version was buried somewhere under the layers. This certainly has something to do with his inability to communicate in English. Whatever Fangio said was filtered through Italian or Argentine journalists who may have found the material lacking in substance and added some padding of their own. One piece of particularly inventive padding was the claim that Fangio had seen Pierre Levegh raise his hand in warning seconds before his death, so saving the Argentinean's life. Not a bad story, certainly.

Despite the tragedy and death toll of 83, the race was not interrupted but continued for another almost 22 hours to complete the full distance. However, during the night, the entire Mercedes team was withdrawn with Fangio/Moss in the lead.

As was to be expected, the disaster brought the world of motor racing into international disrepute for years to come. The general prohibition of motor racing which was issued in Switzerland remains applicable to this day.

So where was Mercedes, with its unbroken supremacy on the racetracks of the era, to go from there? Mercedes helped Fangio to his third World Championship victory, Moss came second. And as the SLRs were also running like a dream, Mercedes even challenged Ferrari in the Sports Car World Championship, actually won the Targa Florio, and so secured themselves that title too.

Perhaps this was just too much of a good thing. At any rate it provided the perfect justification for the Mercedes works team's shock announcement of its intention to pull out at the end of 1955: It had simply won everything there was to win.

At the end of 1955, Gianni Lancia also withdrew his racing team, although not from choice. The Lancia Grand Prix car with its characteristic side tanks was a piece of technical wizardry and would have stood a good chance of dominating the racetracks over the coming years, but the company had overstretched itself and was now faced with the prospect of looming bankruptcy.

So Lancia made a present of the entire Grand Prix technology including cars, components, design drawings, the lot to Enzo Ferrari, who at that time was also swimming in the Formula One sea with no land in sight. Buoyed up by the Lancia inheritance, Ferrari found himself afloat once again and looked round to find the best man he could get hold of. Needless to say, Fangio.

The relationship between Fangio and Enzo Ferrari is another one of those pieces of motor racing history which has been plastered over down the years with layers upon layers of truths and untruths. All that can be squeezed out of Fangio on the subject even today is that: "Ferrari was a great man. We lived through difficult times, but our relationship was nothing but correct."

Words which are typical of the distinguished and wise old man Fangio is today. But still it is fairly safe to assume that the tendency described in an unauthorized Fangio biography published 30 years ago has much of the ring of truth about it. What was at variance was the fact of publishing these details – Fangio himself was always the soul of discretion.

It is easy enough to imagine the rest: The loathing felt by the Argentinean, unbending to the point of stubbornness, for the squabbling for rank and order that went on at the Ferrari court, his distaste for the disgracefully bad manners of the Italian, and his unwillingness to accept, after two years of outstanding Mercedes efficiency, the series of defects to emerge as a result of careless workmanship. And Ferrari, renowned as a scrooge, must have hated Fangio for the simple reason that he was the first not to budge on the matter of fee negotiations. Up to then his line had been that it must be an honor for any pilot to drive for Ferrari. The Argentinean's position was that he had honor enough of his own.

Putting all that aside, the two had come together for the joint purpose of contesting the World Championship against Maserati, and it was thanks to some of those defects that the finale turned out to be an extremely close contest. Although Fangio was winning on points before the last race in Monza, Collins (also Ferrari) and Behra (Maserati) both had a good chance of snatching the title. However much Enzo Ferrari used the proverbial wooden spoon among his team members, he did not pronounce an official pecking order. Fangio had only one declared ally in the team, the sparkling Marquis de Portago. Unfortunately he dropped out almost straight away, leaving Fangio, caught out by one of those defects, stranded in the pit without a car to change into (common practice in those days). Although Luigi Musso was signalled to come in to the pit, he disobeyed the order. Then he came in after all for a tire change, but stayed decidedly put. Fangio stood looking on with an "expressionless face". Next in was Collins, who saw Fangio, jumped out without a moment's hesitation and offered his car to the older man – despite the fact that his own chance for the title was still wide open. Fangio dashed off, came in second behind Moss, and so snatched his fourth World Championship victory.

In 1957, Fangio returned to Maserati. The challenge he now faced came from a rising wave of young drivers, above all the British. Stirling Moss, Mike Hawthorn, Peter Collins, Tony Brooks – all vigorous young men in their twenties to Fangio's 46, the only member of his pre-war generation left. From the technical point of view, too, there were major changes coming: The very first Grand Prix car with a rear engine appeared. The Cooper Climax weighed 375 kilos, heralding a new age of lightweight engineering.

There has never been another racing driver (perhaps with the exception of Senna) with Fangio's intuition, his instinctive ability to make a mark at the right time and leave the rest gaping. Just when they all believed they had the older man where they could beat him most easily, on the old Nürburgring which called for a unique mixture of physical condition, power and reckless driving, Fangio tapped some hidden source and rose above anything they had seen or experienced yet.

After a bungled refueling stop, with almost a minute to make up, Fangio made a lap record out of each one of the last eight laps, taking ten seconds per lap off the Ferraris driven by Hawthorn and Collins, overtook both on the penultimate lap and in 9:17.4 minutes (average speed 147.8 km/h), set up a memorial of a lap record on the still unmodified Nürburgring.

This was his fifth World Championship title.

Around the middle of the 1956 season, Fangio announced his retirement. There was a touch of symbolism about his fourth place in the last race in Reims: In front of him those beaming young men of the generation which was to replace him, Hawthorn, Moss, Trips. We know now only too well what was to be the fate of most of that lost Grand Prix generation: Of those in the World Championship points list in 1958, eight were to die in accidents: Luigi Musso, Peter Collins, Harry Schell, Wolfgang Berghe von Trips, Jean Behra, Joakim Bonnier, Bruce McLaren and – on the open road – Mike Hawthorn, the first World Champion to follow Fangio.

Back to the present, to those gigantic old trees on Fangio's ranch where we sit, miles away from the nearest sign of habitation. Lili makes sure that Fangio takes enough rests, walks up and down with him in the shade. That his state of health is wormwood to those many faithful friends of his is something you cannot help but feel – none of those here are practiced enough in deceit to hide it.

Despite everything, the dignity of Juan Manuel Fangio at the grand old age of 83 radiates with such spontaneity and natural ease that we consciously savor each hour and every single minute in the presence of this man. For a writer, too much respect can be an awful impediment, getting in the way of audacious ideas and allusions.

If asked to sum up in just a few words what it is that makes Fangio the greatest, the answer is twofold. Firstly, it is his complexity as a racing driver which is mentioned again and again in connection with Senna. Both were pilots of the same cast when it came to instinct for the absolute maximum achievable, and for the interplay between all conceivable circumstances: The rigor of the chase, of penetrating the field, to a degree in which individual actions took on the aura of miracles. There existed a special closeness between Fangio and Senna which was not born of coincidence. We know from Fangio's niece about the

old man's dismay as he saw Senna's car crash on the television broadcast. It was only considered safe to tell him Senna was dead later, when there was a doctor close by.

The human phenomenon Fangio is perhaps best expressed in terms of his simplicity. He was the son of a manual worker from way out yonder on the Pampa. He never wanted to be anything else, and never tried to fool anyone into thinking anything different. And he stuck by this simple philosophy through it all, to the dizzy heights of success, through the deepest chaos, in every language, which he never found important enough to want to learn. It was this outstanding clarity of vision which lent him the dignity that shines even from the frail old man he is today. It has filled the cup of his old age with the milk of so much human love and affection that any preconceived idea of the loneliness ofthe aging star is banished without a further thought. He has remained a star, he is cradled in the bosom of his family, his clan, in the very heart of Argentina itself.

Together, we drove back to Mar del Plata.

As we waited on the airstrip for the flight to Buenos-Aires, I asked him on which occasion he believed himself to have been most lucky.

He said: "Sometime during the fifties, I went to the cinema in London, even though I couldn't speak any English. I thought I might understand the film by following the action. I found I couldn't, so I got up halfway through and left. As I got to the door, I heard a tremendous crash: A simply enormous chandelier in the middle of the theater had fallen down. I had been sitting just about exactly underneath it".

MARIE AND CAROLA

Our thoughts turn again to the three points of the Daimler star:
By land, water and air

From a time when progress was synonymous with unpleasant smelling, smoke-belching monstrosities, what an exceedingly attractive monument this is. Marie embodies the pursuit of an elusive vision of design technology, the lady aboard her the generation which has witnessed the fulfillment of that vision: Carola Daimler-Prangen, the great-granddaughter of the genius, who brings the history of that legendary pursuit full circle.

Marie entered the scene in 1988, when Gottlieb Daimler's motto "by land, water and air" helped generate the courage needed to face the many pitfalls that were to delay the breakthrough of the "carriage engine". Daimler was indeed to promote the application of his engine in all three fields (needless to say a suitable flying machine had not yet made its appearance), intending to push forward wherever the market responded most flexibly. And indeed it was the field of boat engines which took off most quickly, making this at one time the backbone of the company.

The milestones along the path of this small, light, high-speed built-in machine, which was bound to follow Nikolaus August Otto's four-stroke engine invention, can be sketched out with relative clarity: 1883 the

Daimler patent, 1885 installation in the new "horseless carriage", 1886 application both as a carriage and a boat engine.

There is no shortage of anecdotes told about those early boat testing sessions on the River Neckar: The fear of the police and of over-officious citizens, the panic displayed in the face of anything to do with petrol and its explosive properties. It was to allay this underlying fear that dummy porcelain knobs wound round with wire were attached to the Marie's railings: Anyone curious enough could conclude these to be insulators and assume the

boat to be driven by electric power. The boat's power unit was a "high-speed" single-cylinder petrol engine with a closed crank case built in a handy grandfather clock-type format which was easily positioned in a boat, and provided more of an ornament than an irritation. With a cubic capacity of 462 cc, it offered up an output of 1.5 horsepower at 700 rpm, which was amply sufficient to propel a boat like the Marie forward at 10 km/h. The "grandfather clock" engine may justly be considered something of a technical sculpture which radiates a strange beauty of its own. It was not

long before the boat was operating, relatively quietly, according to plan on the River Neckar, and nothing happened to arouse undue mistrust among the local population or the police force – something which could not in any way be taken for granted. Gottlieb Daimler made a present of the Marie to Fürst Bismarck – a gesture with all the polish of a modern publicity stunt. Why the boat bore the name it did is the subject of mere conjecture, and the same uncertainty exists as to the frequency with which Bismarck betook himself aboard the Marie: Existing reports range from "never" to "often". In 1922, Bismarck's heirs returned the boat to the Daimler Motor Company.

Carola Daimler-Prangen is Gottlieb Daimler's great-granddaughter, the "Marie" as seaworthy as she was 106 years ago

SPEED MANIA IN AMERICA

BLITZEN BENZ, THE WHITE DINOSAUR FROM THE PREHISTORIC DAYS OF RECORD-EATING AUTOMOBILES:
DAYS WHEN ALL THAT COUNTED WERE ABSOLUTE VALUES AND ULTIMATE PERFORMANCE, WHEN EVERYONE WITNESSING A NEW
RECORD ATTEMPT FELT A PART OF WORLD HISTORY IN THE MAKING

THE BEST KIND of imagination is imagination based on fact. Because the gift of imagination is one many of us have forgotten how to use, turn your mind to a film about America in the nineteen-tens, in a decade when a whole continent was being carried along on an all-pervading wave of enthusiasm for the most powerful automobiles of their age. Here, enthusiasm for the automobile era was unbounded, the thirst for performance on four wheels unquenchable in a way unimaginable in Europe, uninhibited by the prejudices and the chicanery of the old school. Here, there were no invisible boundaries separating serious motor racing from the spectacle and the glamour of the traveling show. Speed and speed alone was the criterion which meant something. And as the fastest automobile was able to beat any railway engine, and of course also the flying machine, all that counted were absolute values, the inconceivable, the superlative. Everyone witnessing a new record attempt felt a part of world history in the making.

Against this background of feverish record-breaking mania came the giant from Germany with its over 20 liter power unit - just imagine the pistons of the 4-cylinder monster - a dinosaur all in white which made noises of a kind never heard by human ear before. Every revolution of the crank or rather every meter driven produced an explosion of a good five liters of gas-air mixture, with a result at the exhaust pipe akin to a battery of artillery fire at close quarters.

The greatest virtue of the pilot was that "he was fearless" and, like his car, a creature of absolutes: Anyone willing to brave this kind of suspension and road holding, to say nothing of the tires, at speeds exceeding 200 km/h, was not a man to be in need of any emotional padding.

The most revered name linked to this white giant was that of 1877-born Barney Oldfield. During his career as a racing cyclist, one of his cycling colleagues teamed up with Henry Ford to try out the new kind of speed experience. The year was 1902, and the vehicle was fitted with 70 horsepower, the most powerful American automobile existing to date: The "999". Henry Ford is quoted as saying: "Tipping yourself over the Niagara Falls was a pure joy compared to a drive in that car". America's first cycling champion also came to the conclusion after his trial run that this was not the type of "speed experience" he had been seeking. His colleague Barney, previously completely unacquainted with the automobile as a form of transport, wasted no time in jumping into his colleague's shoes. He started his driving career by joining a race. Not knowing any better, he simply pressed his foot down on the gas pedal and kept it there. What a natural talent - not only a victory but a new record!

Barney Oldfield was a good-looking young man, was never seen without a casual cigar in his mouth, and turned his "fearless" existence into a sort of trademark. He was at any rate the first racing driver to gain nationwide fame. Although taking part with no small degree of success in

*Circus show fit for an emperor:
The career of the Blitzen Benz was
mapped out by a strange mixture
of ambitious engineering skill,
emotional rapture and pure
sensationalism.
Despite a sectional steel
framework with reinforcing
cross-members and a monster
engine, the car did not exceed
a trim 1 1/2 tons*

serious racing events, as soon as these began to take shape in America, he also joined with great enthusiasm in the showmanship aspect which was gathering momentum in the American motor racing arena. Hardly a day went by without his appearing on some dirt track in the Mid-West, or rising to some challenge or another set up with all the choreographed perfection of a wrestling tournament: fierce rivalry, desperate dueling and action unlimited - all with a predictable outcome, and all involving cars.

Towards the end of the first decade of the century, a second racing driver personality entered stage right with a whole fistful of track records: Ralph de Palma, who was primarily a Fiat man. The encounter between the two rival stars in a King Kong versus Godzilla battle for the absolute speed record was the ultimate hit of all conceivable scenarios in the American motor racing world at the time. The Manager of the Oldfield Troupe in 1910 secured the legendary new Benz for the occasion while it was still making its way over the Atlantic. To capture the wrestling spirit which pervaded the better tournaments, the car needed a "nom de guerre", which was coined with the Lightning Benz. While the car was still on American soil, the Germanized version of its name, "Blitzen Benz", somehow made itself popular - a development which was taken up with some gratitude back home in Germany, at that time in the hey-day of the Kaiser era.

The company Benz would itself never have stooped to christen its offspring with such an appendage: The project had been launched with the same serious sense of undertaking that applied to everything the company did. In its rivalry with its competitors, in particular with the Daimler-Motoren-Gesellschaft, Benz had only been tempted to enter the motor rac-

ing arena on a few rare occasions. Karl Benz himself had no time for racing at all. He considered all proposals aimed at increasing speed anywhere in excess of 50 km/h to be "nonsense". In view of the highly "mixed traffic" abroad on the roads around the turn of the century, this was wisdom indeed. However, with every passing year of the new century, the importance attributed to motor racing success grew, in particular for those most serious of manufacturers, and after two half-hearted racing involvements, Benz entered the fray on a serious basis in 1908.

Aided by a team of highly committed specialists put together practically overnight, the company managed to bridge the first season of its participation very respectably, and came up with some superb Grand Prix cars in compliance with the regulations then applicable, whose only limitation was a maximum bore of 155 mm. Anyone with enough imagination and the courage of his convictions could take a 200 mm stroke to produce a 15 liter four-cylinder engine. That is just what Benz did. The car's performance at the major European venues of 1908 was spectacular although adverse circumstances prevented it from gaining overall victory. In a bid to extract the full benefit of the high development costs, participation in the American circuits appeared an opportunity too good to be missed. The New York importer was more than helpful with the arrangements. So it came about that, in 1909, a Benz Grand Prix car fell into the hands of Barney Oldfield, who showed off its paces for example in Indianapolis (before the days of the legendary 500 mile race, which started in 1911).

The sheer potential offered by this hit combination led to an ever greater increase in record-breaking mania on both sides of the Atlantic. As an American steam car had, in the meantime, broken the 200 km/h barrier,

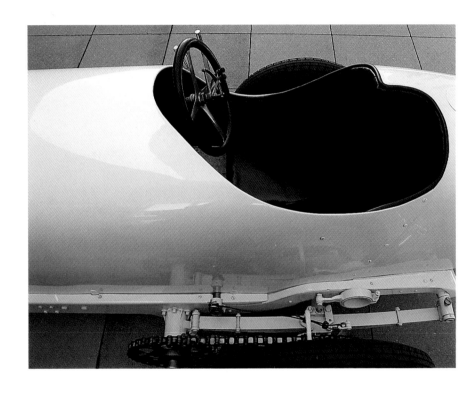

Power transmission using the shortest route according to the bicycle principle. Final ratio was regulated using a selection of chain wheels

drastic action was called for: The bore was increased to 185 mm, resulting in a cubic capacity of more than 21 liters, or 21.504 cc to be exact. Output was said to amount to precisely 200 bhp at 1600 rpm. Other contemporary findings were naturally integrated in a bid to increase speed: a pointed rear end and narrower bodywork cross-section. As the car was to be used for shorter distances, there was no need to face the problem of efficient cooling over long periods, and this wonderfully narrow, high radiator was sufficient. A highly functional detail, the ideally streamlined configuration of the upper edge of the radiator, which formed a sort of beak, also added a touch of the aggressive to the appearance.

This new model was to become known as the Blitzen Benz, with Barney Oldfield ready to take the wheel.

The speed enthusiasts on both sides of the Atlantic had, by this time, already come to the realization that even a brand-new race track was in fact an impediment to the achievement of maximum actually possible speeds. The models which were being newly developed for speed could not be stretched to their limits even on tracks with specially designed cambers, as the progress which was taking place on the engine front was only marginally matched by developments to vehicle chassis and general road holding. What was needed were long, flat stretches. The compacted sand strip of Daytona Beach came into its own long before motor racing discovered Salt Lake. The breathlessly awaited encounter between Ralph de Palma (Fiat) and Barney Oldfield (Benz) which was due to take place in March 1910 fell flat, for reasons which have long since filtered through the quicksands of the archives. Opponent or no, Oldfield was not one to miss such an opportunity and turned up for the waiting reporters. In yet another

record-breaking attempt, he achieved a speed of just under 212 km/h with apparent ease. Formal irregularities prevented the speed from being officially recorded, but nobody was denying that the Blitzen Benz from Germany was the fastest thing on four wheels to date.

The unbridled enthusiasm of the American public for all things connected with speed during that memorable era guaranteed the partnership "Barney Oldfield" and "Blitzen Benz" a place in the Hall of Fame: This was the most exciting pair to take to the tarmac in those heady early years of motor racing, an American legend.

To add to the aggressor image cultivated for the pair, the white Benz was adorned with the Kaiser's coat of arms, and the effect was perfect. The show took to the road.

Towards the end of 1910, the ruling sports authorities drew a line under this mixture of sport and circus and banned Barney Oldfield from appearing - at least from those venues and race tracks where they had any say. Barney and his troupe took a detour to Mexico to return with a slightly damaged although reparable Blitzen Benz. Still at loggerheads with the sports authorities, Oldfield was out of the question as a driver for the official record-beating event held in Daytona in the spring of 1911, giving a

Space for two: The poor devil of a co-pilot sat further back. The gear shift and hand brake lever were located outside the bodywork. The aggressive beak fulfilled a practical purpose: to accommodate the tank for the extremely narrow, high radiator

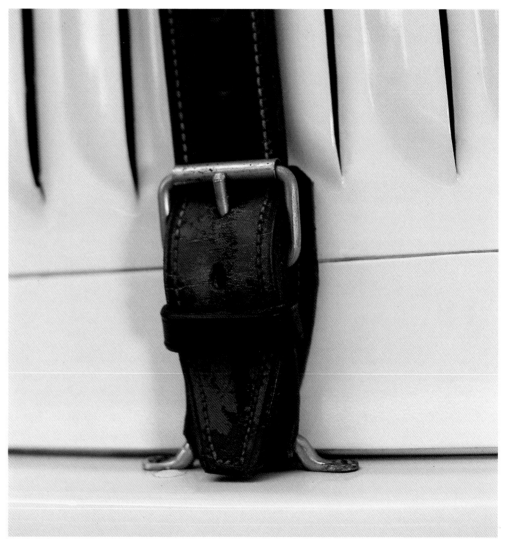

EVERYTHING BAR FLYING

THE LAST RECORD-BREAKING CAR
WHICH STILL ALLOWED THE LUXURY OF A FRIENDLY PAIR OF NOSTRILS

THIS IS WHAT IT LOOKED LIKE, a good, respectable record-breaking car built using the solid foundation of accepted racing automobile technology. The record-breaking fever of the thirties also produced monstrosities sporting 2,500 bhp (Campbell's "Bluebird", for instance), which broke the 500 km/h barrier and announced their intention of going for the big 600. Even Mercedes let itself be swept along in the speed mania, installing a 2,800 bhp aircraft engine (12 cylinders, 44 litres cubic capacity) into one of Ferdinand Porsche's constructions, but the war put an abrupt stop to the project before the terrifying spectre of the T80 ever put tire to tarmac.

So it happened that for Mercedes, these "record-breaking years" remain linked to the names Caracciola and von Brauchitsch, the modified W25 and W125 racing cars, and the frenzied excitement of those memorable duels with Auto Union, whipped to a frenzy by the general "Germany!" mania of those pre-war days.

The most memorable day of that age was January 28th, 1938, when Caracciola set a new record of 432.7 km/h on the Frankfurt - Darmstadt Autobahn in a 5.6-litre 12-cylinder. As a class record (5 - 8 litre engines), this was to remain unbroken for a quarter of a century, and on the public highway it still stands. That the autobahn was not built to support speeds of this order was tragically brought home on that same January day in 1938, when Bernd Rosemeyer (Auto Union) met his death on the same stretch.

His Auto Union had reached a speed of 450 km/h when he crashed near Mörfelden. There were no eye witnesses who could have testified whether his car had been swept out of control by a gust of side wind, or whether a more complex phenomenon was at work as Mr. Neubauer, head of racing at Mercedes, suspected: The wind resistance pressure was increased by the side wind from a clearing to an extent that the thin aluminium panelling was unable to withstand it. The bodywork of the car buckled under the strain, so losing its streamlining effect, consequently buckled even further and finally shattered. Neubauer: "It was as if the car had hit a wall at 450 km/h."

Whatever the truth of the matter: Using conventional technology, and presuming the record-breaking car to represent a stage in the evolution of the racing car, the absolute achievable limit had been reached. The "Avus" W25 depicted on these pages represents the very last stage of this all-round development process (even the closely related Caracciola record car from 1938 had crossed a decisive barrier by making use not of a conventional radiator but of a short term ice cooling system, allowing the two front air intake slits to be done away with, which had a decisive aerodynamic impact at speeds upwards of 400 km/h like the difference between flying and driving).

The 1937 car (W 25 streamline "Avus"), which henceforth bore the number 36 as a permanent feature, was certainly suited for racing with a

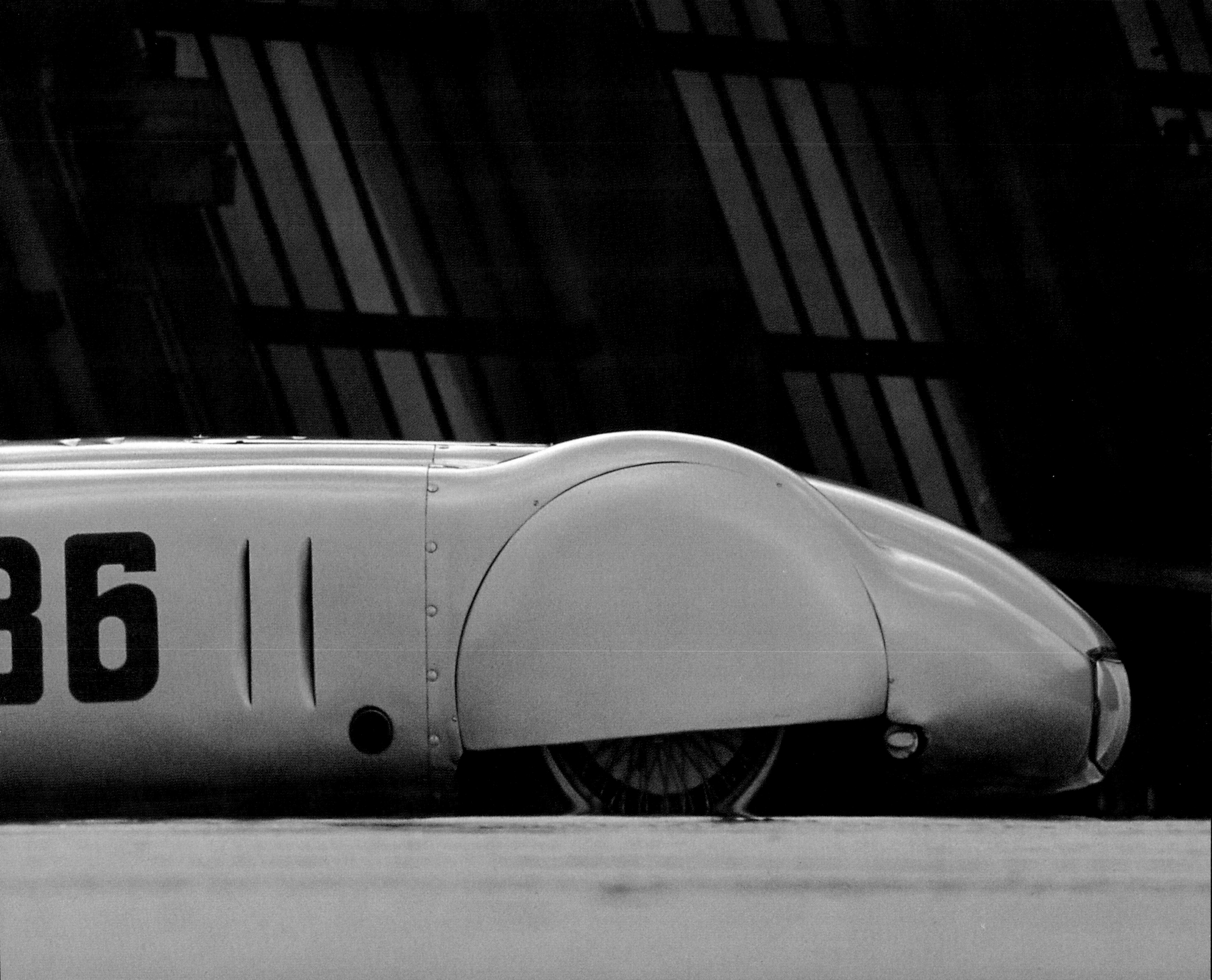

The ultimate stage of the joint evolution between the Grand Prix and the record-breaking car. Thanks to a 5.5 litre twelve-cylinder engine, the "Avus"-W25 achieved a speed of 372 km/h on the basis of proven racing car engineering

twelve-cylinder engine (5.576 cc, 756 bhp at 5,800 revs), if only on the Avus track in Berlin with its extremely long straights. After extension work on the high-speed north loop, in 1937 the track saw the fastest races of all time: The average speeds of 276 km/h (fastest lap) and 261 km/h (overall race average of the winner) outmatch anything conceivable on today's Grand Prix tracks. "Number 36" piloted by Manfred von Brau-

chitsch won the second qualifying run, and dropped out with a technical defect in the main heat.

And when it came to pure speed, the "Avus" achieved 372 km/h – with conventional radiator and those friendly nostrils, an abomination to all aerodynamics experts and drag coefficient chasers.

SWING

THIS CAR CANNOT in all honesty be claimed as one of central importance to Mercedes history. In terms of piece numbers it is a small fry indeed, its technical standard is in keeping with the generally elevated demands and expectations of its day, and in historical terms, too, there is nothing monumental that it can be said to have achieved.

What it gives us is a prime example of the way in which an era turned the achievement of style and beauty into an end unto itself, in which crocodile tears shed for the "unnecessary" and the "nonfunctional" were just so much water under the bridge, in which the sole aim was pure aesthetics for its own sake.

The central feature from which the style of the car radiates is the fender: Its bold sweep suggestive of the enormous power which may be lurking under the engine cowling (while in actually it contains a tame six-cylinder), trailing off into a running board, and rising to form a neat and sober enclosure for the rear wheel, playfully drawing attention from the ugly mounted rear trunk and breaking up the unfavourable proportions of the rear end. The design is the typical expression of the early thirties, and was to be followed by still more dramatically sweeping wings, particularly coming from the French coachbuilders. However, these later models were already affected by the new streamlining euphoria which was beginning to exert an ever greater influence on designers, inducing them to chop away elegant fender skirts and chisel rear ends into ugly points.

The fender as a functional piece of automobile hardware turned into the wing, an elegantly sweeping ornamental feature which slotted comfortably into the jazz era, to the swinging interpretation of its functional self. This new swing also lent itself to the fluidity of the border line between the elegant sports car and the elegant touring car. The defining line between the terms became blurred and indistinct.

As far as its appearance was concerned, the Mannheim Convertible could have passed as a Bugatti anytime, and its similarity to the Grand Sport Coupé Bugatti Type 55, Jean Bugatti's masterpiece (son of Ettore), is astounding. As both cars came out at practically the same time, in 1931, no questions were ever asked about who might possibly have filched ideas from the other: This special arrangement, this enigmatic sweep was simply the tangible proof that great minds really do think alike.

One of the fundamental differences between the Bugatti Coupé and the Mannheim Convertible lay in its hidden character. The French model was a racing car got up to resemble a touring car, its engine (eight cylinders with supercharger) offered up the 125 hp which would have been expected at Grand Prix level. This man-of-war engine lent the car a more serious note, and what we could be justified in calling the moral right to parade a magnificent hood of these proportions.

The Mannheim offered a plainer diet beneath its shining bodywork. A nifty but non-supercharged six-cylinder engine produced just 75 horse-

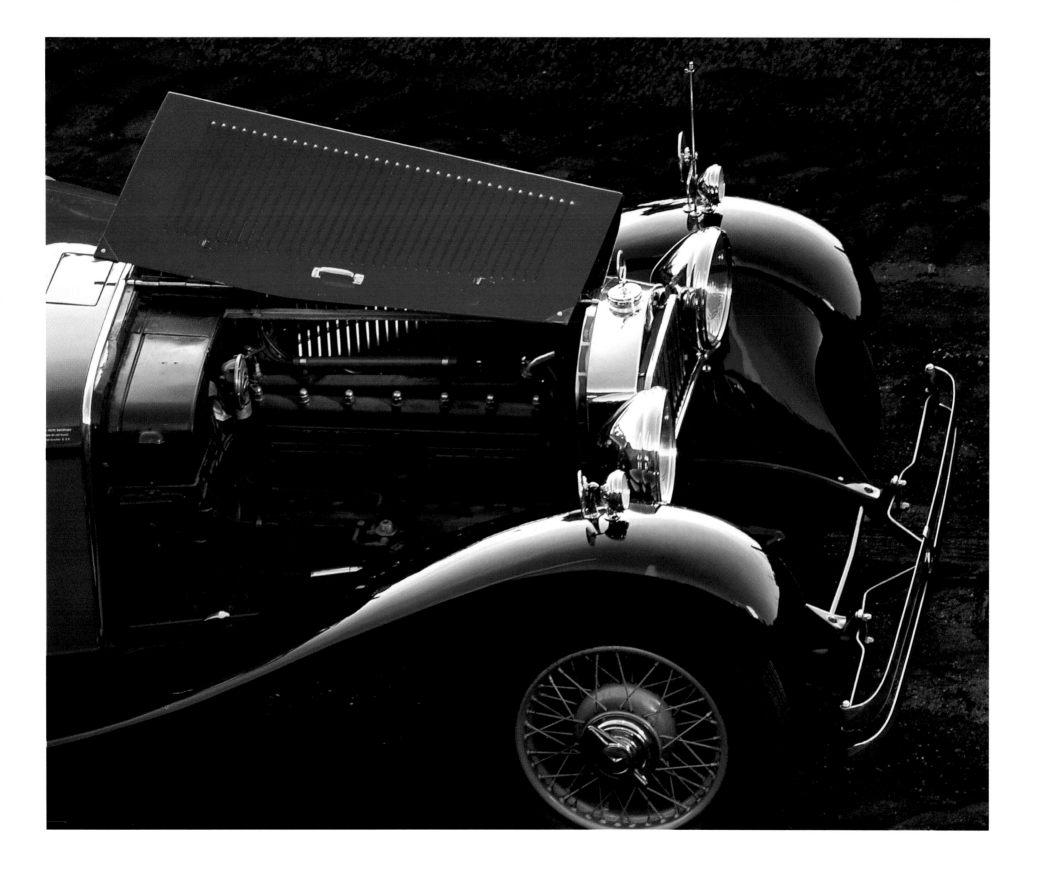

power – and in other ways, too, this model really fitted into the upper end of the executive class range, an "economical six-seater" in bird-of-paradise plumes. The Mannheim series was one of the new models designed by Porsche successor Hans Nibel to be launched following the merger of Daimler with Benz, and model names like Stuttgart and Mannheim were symbolic of the fusion and the new feeling of togetherness.

This 370 S version which so dramatically outshone the basic Mannheim model was, at any rate, an object of desire for all those who would have liked to be able to afford more horses in their stable but lacked the necessary economic muscle. And one thing we should make no bones about: As far as the sweeping wing was concerned, the 370 S had nothing to blush about even next to the most superb SS versions.

The bare facts did not offer quite so much to get worked up about as the sheer aesthetics: 75 horsepower for a car weighing 1600 kilos.
Between 1931 and 1933, 183 of the 370 S were built, representing around a tenth of the entire Mannheim series ever produced

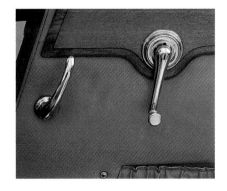

ON THE WRONG TRACK...

THE SHIFT BETWEEN THE THIRD AND FOURTH GEARS IS PARTICULARLY AMENABLE... STRAIGHT OUT OF THE WONDERFUL
WORLD OF ADVERTISING LITERATURE. THE TYPE 150 WAS THE MOST CONVINCING WAY TO TALK PEOPLE INTO ACCEPTING THAT THE
ENGINE DOES NOT ALWAYS HAVE TO BE AT THE FRONT IN A MERCEDES.
BUT DID ANYONE REALLY WANT TO KNOW?

HOW BEST TO PRESENT A CAR which was not only costly but also featured a technical concept previously accepted exclusively - and only grudgingly - for use in smaller vehicles? No easy task indeed to persuade people that what had always been taken as a drawback was in fact an immense technical benefit with a little faith and a little moderation driving round corners. Perhaps the best way was simply to play the whole subject down, to neatly sidestep the question with a few discreet niceties? Something like this, perhaps:

"In the Mercedes-Benz Type 150, the benefits of the utility car combine ideally with the amenities of a sports vehicle. The owner derives the full benefit achieved by this combination of characteristics: The Type 150 offers high motoring performance as well as outstanding economy, and is easy to maintain and handle.

"If we take a closer look at the special performance offered by this model in the light of its intended application, the most striking aspects are its power of acceleration and its outstanding top speed. The explanation for these features lies not only in the surprisingly high peak output of the engine, an overhead valve 4-cylinder offering 55 bhp with a cubic capacity of only 1.5 liters, but also particularly in the excellent weight to output ratio, with one hp propelling only 19 kg! This is the secret behind the superb acceleration offered in every gear, lending the car an almost sup-

ercharged effect. This characteristic alone is enough to categorize the Type 150 as an out-and-out sportscar, which provides immediate evidence of outstanding performance and makes it a distinguished representative of its class.

"The engine performance is complemented by the general handling properties which are little short of amazing for a sports car, and are perhaps best explained by the Mercedes-Benz Type 150's close ties to the world-renowned Daimler-Benz AG swing axle range. Thanks to patent-protected swing axles front and rear, correct weight distribution and a wide track width, the Type 150 offers impressive road holding, which comes into its own particularly on poor road surfaces and in tight corners. Whatever the condition of the road, the car drives safely and free of vibrations notwithstanding potholes or other surface unevenness. The fact that each of the four wheels is able to position itself independently of the other three, and so adapt individually to road conditions, lends the Type 150 a remarkably safe cornering action. It is the successful combination of impressive engine performance and amazing road holding that determine the outstanding benefit of this car, making it not just a sports car but also - thanks to its generous luggage compartment - a useful high-speed touring car which leaves nothing to be desired in terms of sporting driving enjoyment.

"Clearly, in a vehicle of this caliber there are certain basic conditi-

It was called the "150", but its real name was "Heck", i.e. "stern", "tail", "rear", short for "rear engine". The technical motto left all sorts of scope for stylistic expression, the double wheel composition reinforced the rear-ward emphasis

ons to be fulfilled. These include not only engine performance and handling, but also various safety aspects.

"First and foremost, particular care must be given to the choice of materials. Only the very best of the best was good enough, and every conceivable expedient testing method was undertaken to achieve a reassuring standard of safety during construction of the car. The use of the swing axles represents a further particularly important safety factor which exerts a considerable influence not only on handling characteristics in general, but also on the car's braking capacity. The Mercedes-Benz Type 150 is equipped with a hydraulic brake which has a soft but persistent response sufficient to bring the vehicle to a standstill within a few meters in emergencies. The action of the brake is supported by continuous contact of the four wheels with the road due to the individual suspension, which ensures one hundred percent braking effectiveness.

"For the sporting driver, the car offers two other particularly important points to note: Firstly the simplicity of operation, and secondly the cooling system. As for the former, drivers should bear in mind that fast and easy operation of vehicle functions plays an extremely important role in any motor racing or other competitive events. This aspect received particular attention during the design and construction of the car. The independent wheel suspension operates completely smoothly, the wheels are guided with absolute accuracy and lightness by the movements of the steering wheel while still maintaining road contact. To allow the driver to keep his hands on the wheel while signaling, a handy horn actuating ring is mounted on the steering wheel itself, which allows a signal to be given in any position of the steering wheel. The driving ease offered by the car also includes operation of the four forward gears and reverse. The gear shift is light and noiseless, the gear shift lever arranged for comfortable operation. The shift between the third and fourth gears (top speed) is particularly amenable: The gear is changed simply by shifting the lever and releasing the accelerator. There is no need to apply the clutch, the top speed and third gears engage automatically. The top speed reduces en-gine revolutions at high speeds, so relieving the strain on all sections of the power unit: A particular benefit for the driver on long journeys and when traveling at high speeds.

"The radiator of this car presents a particularly interesting solution. While previous conventional arrangements did not permit projection beyond a certain radiator depth, due to technical progress it is now possible to fit a radiator of any optional depth. This new possibility means that the radiator, whose size depends on engine performance, can now be designed to suit the given spatial conditions irrespective of any limiting height or width. The basic functional principle of the Type 150 radiator involves a high-performance turbine which takes in cold air from the outside and compresses it at high speed through the honeycomb radiator. This system provides an extensive and, above all, reliable dissipation of heat. The other special benefits of this cooling system are that a blower of this type uses less energy than the conventional fan and that noise is cut to a minimum.

"As the Type 150 is designed as a true two-seater model, the engine is arranged towards the back in front of the rear axle, and forms an integral unit with the transmission, clutch and rear axle casing. The superb access afforded to all components, in particular the carburetor, valves, spark plugs and other essential parts is particularly worthy of note. This benefit is one which will be welcomed especially by all drivers taking part

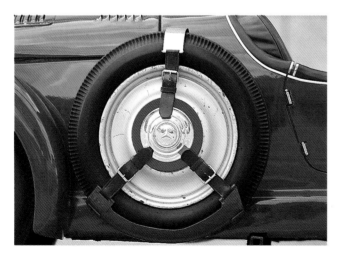

The car's
beauty expressed
itself mostly from its
silhouette, but its
closed countenance
was the most
astounding styling
element of all.
So much so that the
designers were at a
loss to know quite
what to do with
their new-won
freedom

in competitive events.

"The convenient W.V.oil-shot lubrication relieves the driver of troublesome greasing of individual lubrication points. The lubrication system supplies all the car's lubrication points automatically with fresh oil simply by pressing a pedal, also while traveling. The helical springs on the rear axle are mounted using a jointless technique, and therefore require no maintenance.

"The valuable operating experience gathered with ten thousand Mercedes-Benz swing axle cars already in circulation, a large number of fundamental patents, especially in the field of rear engine car construction and the result of 50 years of practical involvement in the construction of high-performance sports cars also form the basis for the design and appointments of this new Mercedes-Benz model. The result is an all-around mature sports car subjected to thorough and stringent testing which is reasonable in price, a vehicle whose manifold qualities are both impressive and convincing! "

This sales brochure, published in 1934, was clearly very reticent about singing the praises of its rear engine concept, and kept the fact that the engine had already been shifted slightly forward, almost to the position of a mid-engine, relatively quiet. This move initially left the small 130 model, planned for mass production and sale, as the only one with what could still be strictly seen as a rear engine. The swan which was supposed to cultivate the ugly duckling went about the task in a very half-hearted manner. And as a model in its own right, the 150 sport roadster remained something of a fruitless exercise. It simply did not sell, and only five cars were ever built. Seen in historical retrospect, the Type 150 is relegated to the ranks of the exciting and in many aspects highly successful styling study.

The objective had been to unite the streamlining craze of the age with the practical details of the "Volkswagen" or "people's car" idea, which was then in its infancy.

Practical details, the Volkswagen idea - these are key concepts which apply to the major model of the series, the 130. Opinions diverge about just how directly the stock of ideas contributed by Ferdinand Porsche (employed with Mercedes up until 1928) were connected with the construction of the first rear engine prototypes at Mercedes (1931), which served as a basis for the 130 series from 1934 onwards. At any rate, the hot topic of the day among the designers was to have another attempt at making use of low-cost backyard workshop technology involving the shortest possible drive paths for use in "real cars". Mercedes was the first producer to take the courageous step in this direction on a grand scale.

Added to this was the enthusiasm which greeted what was, after all, the first "small car" (405 cm) ever to be produced at Mercedes. The excitement was based more on optical aspects than technical ones. The streamlining, pointed rear end and "beetle" elements which emerge clearly in the prototype development were only partially adopted for the series vehicle. Instead, the 130 had all the insignia of a mature utility car. The shape of the frontal structure could just as easily have concealed the radiator and engine, the lack of air inlets was the only really new, admittedly exciting, "styling element". The conventional interpretation served up by the company in describing what was in effect a new automobile philosophy is indicative of lacking confidence in its new rear-engined development.

The accommodation of luggage, the comfort (all four seats located between the two axles providing "considerably improved convenience") and in particular the "incomparable handling characteristics" were highlighted with all possible eloquence, as were the "soft, gliding drive" provided by the swing axles, which were brought very successfully to bear in this vehicle configuration.

It was with the one-to two-thirds weight distribution that the "incomparable" nature of the handling characteristics took on a meaning of its own. The rear end frequently forced its way to the forefront, particularly on fast corners - which made even the delicate 1300 engine with its 26 bhp amply sufficient.

And there were, of course, customers whose driving habits precluded any of this type of symptom - and who consequently had no hesitation in declaring their satisfaction about the undemanding character of their 130, its light steering and its relative spaciousness. To nip the creeping doubts that were beginning to grow in its own ranks firmly in the bud, the central publicity bureau snatched with enthusiasm at any such reports that came their way and sent copies circulating around the company. While the accompanying notes sent with these during the first year of the rear-engined series (1934) still contained attempts at friendly motivation ("as you may see for yourself, our smallest Mercedes-Benz is meeting with ever greater popularity at home and abroad: A circumstance which should inspire you with enthusiasm when it comes to sales and publicity!"), by the following year the tone of these epistles had become several degrees more dramatic:"We urge you not to rest and to leave no stone unturned until your entire sales staff takes up the ideas contained in this letter of acknowledgment and has become convinced that this type of positive customer appraisal is the best possible instrument to eliminate all existing prejudice. We repeat once again that it is only in the firm conviction of the superiority and quality of our rear-engined model on the part of all the gentlemen of our sales force that we may be sure of success. It should be a matter of course that the same unconditional conviction expressed by the customer in his assessment should be forthcoming from our own ranks."

Obviously all to no avail, as in the following year the sales figures plummeted. The follow-on rear-engined model (with markedly better handling characteristics) was launched at the same time as an equivalent front-engined model. The difference between the 170 H and its front-engined equivalent the 170 V took such dramatic proportions that the whole rear-engine episode was put down to experience and shelved indefinitely.

*The elegant but
practically unsaleable
swan came with this
utilitarian ugly duckling
in tow: The small
rear-engined Type 130
which entered series
production in 1934*

TURNING THE CLOCK BACK

Celebration of a memory or invocation of an unlived dream:
The trek up the Klausen Pass for all those willing to brave the mountain

Weather's not looking so good after all". The landlady's face is all consternation as she squints up at the clouds which are gathering while I gulp back my morning coffee. On the table is a copy of the local paper "Fridolin", which has appeared in a resplendent 24-page special edition in honor of this very special day.

Here in the Glarnerland area, a good hour's drive west of Zurich, the locals only learn two historical dates: The "Rütli Oath" back in 1291 which marked the foundation of Switzerland, and the "Klausen Memorial" in 1993.

The renaissance of this famous mountain race on the Klausen Pass took place after an extended break of 59 years. Something for full-blood-ed lads with enough of the adventurer in them to follow the tracks of such intrepid early heroes as Caracciola, Stuck, Chiron and Nuvolari, who made Klausen racing history here between 1922 and 1934.

Nothing is missing. The nostalgia. The bizarreness of it all. The motor racing atmosphere. It even smells the way it did, the air vibrates to the droning of lovingly preserved vintage eight and twelve-cylinder engines.

The first relay of participants has already been waiting for hours at the starting line in Linthal, a jumbled mass of over 400 classical automobiles and motorcycles dating back to the twenties and thirties.

The whole town and even the region is up and doing, there is no-one who does not identify with this very special event. The roads have been decorated, the shop windows lovingly adorned with all manner of vintage memorabilia, a band has been playing in the specially erected marquee for days already.

"Anyone who isn't here today is missing out on a once-in-a-life-time experience", is the decided opinion of one participant from

Zurich, only half the age of his 1932 MG. Beaming, he continues: "I have just swept out the displacement - now let's get started!". No, his girlfriend decided to stay away, the excitement would be

The Market Square at Glarus had waited 59 long years for the racing cars to return

too much for her. The course is not without its risks, after all.

At weekends, so the papers say, the locals drive themselves into the ground over the pass. Too bad if his car should perish in the attempt; it would leave a big gap in his life.

A slight break in the threatening bank of clouds over the nearby

mountain gives some grounds for hope of better things to come, but it makes sense to opt for a local store's offer of cut-price umbrellas at only 13 Francs apiece.

At the press conference held in a school yard, a venerable Swiss gentleman in a wheelchair, still full of energy, grows animated as he tells waiting journalists how he won the 500 cc motorcycle class on the Klausen in 1927. The oldest participant to be braving this year's adventure is 83, and is at the wheel of a Bugatti.

And if he should drive it into the ground, it could be worse: This elderly pilot owns a whole museum full of no fewer than 120 vintage cars, including a whole list of Bugattis.

The press bus which is to transport the journalists up to the top of the pass at 2,000 meters above sea level fails to show up. The course has long been shut off to all other traffic. A sprint towards police and ambulances ensues as journalists tussle to find a way to the top. Photographer Peter Vann must have had some sort of premonition: At two in the morning, armed with a thermos of coffee and several pullovers, he had started off on the journey and spent the rest of the night shivering in his car until he was rudely awoken at the crack of dawn by a mountain farmer cursing him for blocking the route up to his cow herd. Once he had fi-

"To stand by the side of a car like this in such a historical spot is an indescribable sensation." (Peterheinz Kern)

Mercedes 680 S built in 1927

nally settled himself in a good strategic position on the slope, the chain of mountain peaks with their candyfloss topping in the background, the breathtaking panorama of winding curves in the foreground, the fog descended. But at least he was up there. Down below in the town, the sun puts in a token appearance, only to give way to another bank of threatening clouds, and the first raindrops are felt. I join forces with a Swiss family - a man, his wife, and two children, who are aiming to ascend the Urnerboden. This 1,500 meter-high vantage point and the biggest, most beautiful grazing mountain in Switzerland should provide a superb view of the lengthy straight along which Caracciola in his Mercedes swept at an impressive 200 km/h in the last Klausen race to be held back in 1934, to set up a never-to-be beaten record time of 15 minutes, 22.2 seconds.

We set off. Still time to turn back. The head of the family, Rüdi by name, had been involved in the organization of the big event. It had actually been necessary to found a company to fight a two-year battle with the authorities and then to complete a further two years of planning. Nowadays it is almost like moving heaven and earth to obtain a permit for any sort of motor racing event. And in such a stronghold of the nature conservationists like the Alps. But even the Green Parties turned a blind eye for this particular event. They may have a whole list of objections to modern cars, but who can bring themselves to condemn a 60 year-old veteran? Nowhere is nostalgic Zeitgeist more outwardly in evi-

dence than when it comes to those shiny, resplendent vintage cars. One of the most difficult hurdles proved to be the mountain farmers, who feared for their pastures and the reaction of their cows' stomachs to a diet of empty cigarette packets or metal tabs from discarded lemonade cans.

Finally, a big question mark hung over the logistics problem. Over the 21.5 kilometer pass with zero infrastructure, stands to accommodate 25,000 had to be set up with the usual trimmings: crossings, fencing, kiosks, toilets and all the rest of it.

17,000 have arrived without polluting the environment by rail and - especially for the occasion - in ancient post office buses, paying the original 1934 fare. Anyone determined to travel in their own car has had to pay 90 dollars for the privilege. The crowd is held in check on either side of the road by 600 helpers and course judges, six rescue teams are stationed at the ready, fire brigades, helicopters and all.

Technology Rudolf Carraciola put his trust in all those years ago

An enormous caravan of spectators begins to clamber over shiny wet gravel up the slope. It is incredibly slippery underfoot, people are stumbling all around us. Behind me, someone scrambles back onto their feet, muttering that it is hardly surprising they call this the "Klausen Memorial": "It isn't something I'm going to forget in a hurry".

On the way up I make the acquaintance of a German from near Lörrach, a real vintage car enthusiast whose prize collection is made up of a single white Eldorado Cadillac standing at home in his garage: A '59 model, the one with the high fins at the back. It is always filled with gas, he tells me, and when his old lady makes life hard for him, in he gets and away he drives. Women you can

avid reader: The small and select family of vintage racing dignitaries was there as a man - Swiss millionaires, French industrialists, English Lords, German nobles. Graf Hubertus Dönhoff, for example, whose estate lies somewhere near Munich, black waistcoat, cigarette in his mouth, dreamy eyes observing the proceedings from under a tousled mane of hair. Now and again the Graf reached for his wine glass containing a dry "Pierrafeu" which he deposited on the radiator of his 1936 Alfa Romeo.

**A Maserati should only be red –
the 6C-32 piloted by Jost Wildbolz**

France, to finally draw up in front of the Hotel Raben in Linthal. The only mechanical breakdowns they had to deal with were caused by the Range Rover that accompanied them.

A racing track of precisely 21.5 kilometers up to the top of the pass at 1937 meters, garnished with more than its fair share of hairpins

find by the dozen, but a car like that only once in a lifetime! I stop for a breather in a clearing and give a little thought to what I might possibly be able to write about a race which I may not even get to see. Amplified by the resonating walls of the mountains, the distant singing of superchargers and the growl of engines are audible. True, the day before in the "parc fermé", the driver's enclosure, I have already witnessed plenty to interest the

"Get in", called Roger Saul of the fashion house of Mulberry, whose unmistakably English-style outfit matches the whole vintage scene to a tee. Mulberry is one of the race's sponsors. For Roger, the epitome of the eccentric but affable Brit in a loud-colored waistcoat and matching Bermudas, business and pleasure are inseparably rolled into one. It took him three days to pilot his '34 wine-red Alfa Spider plus family from British soil, cutting across

Before the big race: Beauty pageant

On top of the world: Peterheinz Kern and the Mercedes 680 S, restored with a meticulous eye to detail

My goodness, what a sensation, to sweep through the town in this racing beauty with its filigree thin legs, the cover down, your body paled into insignificance behind the luxuriously instrumented cockpit, your arm resting casually on the door frame. Only recently, someone had offered him 1.8 million pounds to relinquish his pride and joy. Its very scarcity, the refined pedigree and the indescribable Alfa feeling make this a collector's item of a rare breed indeed.

And on the subject of that Alfa feeling: One hour previously a young BBC reporter had returned with a somewhat green complexion and wobbly legs. He had made the mistake of accompanying Roger on one of his flying training sessions along the course: 21.5 kilometers, 26 right-hand bends, 84 minor corners, and the long straight up on the high plateau, the jumping wheels testing out every groove and every pot hole and passing the message along to the passengers' backbones.

Anyone, like Roger, who is going for the record, has no leisure to worry his head about pedestrian chickens and spectators. He pays no attention to his speed, simply bent on reaching his destination in the shortest possible time. Seen from the roadside perspective, his progress looks like a continuous series of near misses.

From here, there are only eight kilometers to go to the top of the pass. But what those eight kilometers entail! The road winds its way up the mountainside like a giant serpent, the drivers race up hell for leather at 150 km/h, oblivious of the rock face on the right, the deadly drop on their left, sometimes only the sky and a shaky fence before them, sometimes not even that. An oil patch on the road, a burst tire... it does not bear thinking about. Roger Saul returns beaming with delight. Nobody had been in any doubt that the route through these beautiful surroundings would be exciting - but nobody was prepared for just how spectacular it really would really be.

The air becomes noticeably thinner, your heart begins to pound

**A crowd of 25,000 came to pay tribute
to 450 vintage motor cycles and automobiles**

overtime, and in your ears you hear the ringing of countless cowbells. At last we arrive on the Urnerboden. It begins to thunder. A persistent drizzle sets in. Real honest-to-goodness Klausen weather. Nobody lets it dampen the generally high spirits. It drizzles down with unerring regularity on the meticulously tended leather seat covers and polished wooden instrument panels of the Bugattis and Delahaye convertibles which pass us at regular intervals of around a minute. In their old-fashioned leather bomber jackets, leather driving hats and goggles, some of the pilots look and drive as though they are out on a Sunday picnic outing. One

puffs away comfortably at a pipe, another has a co-pilot with him who is busy capturing the whole event on video.

Whatever rattled, thundered or creaked past was greeted with cheers from the crowd: "Faster, faster" is heard on all sides. One man in the crowd bellows out: "A Mercedes!" As a man, the spectators crane their necks to catch a glimpse, mothers hold up their children to get a better look. "He's in a hurry all right", comments one young girl, looking with longing at the grandiose bodywork of the white 680 S Mercedes dating back to 1927.

It was just this very model, with chassis number 35203 and engine number 60410, that hailed a whole new era of racing successes for the Stuttgart producer: This was a car from the first series of only eight vehicles which was to be driven by driving genius Rudolf Caracciola to his very first victory on the occasion of the opening race on the Nürburgring on June 19, 1927.

Over a period of several decades, this car had been given up for lost after being sold to a buyer in America at the beginning of the thirties. Detailed research carried out in Stuttgart and other archives indicated that the car had first been purchased privately by Caracciola before being sold to a new owner abroad.

From then on, this jewel of automotive history appeared to have disappeared without trace. It was at the end of the seventies that the car was discovered, rotting and rusting, in a shed in a back yard in New York. At the time of its discovery, though, no-one was aware of the historic significance of this rusting wreck. The car was bought by an American restorer and renovated to the extent that it could be sold to a buyer in Europe, where it was eventually to end up in the possession of one Peterheinz Kern.

With an incredible eye for the finest, most minute details, Kern took the complete restoration of the Nürburgring winner into his own competent hands. Which takes us on to the next story, to the collector and personality Peterheinz Kern, and another — shall we say — appealing automobile.

KERN'S-CABRIOLET

THE COOL DISCIPLINED STYLING OF THE UNMISTAKABLE SINDELFINGEN BODYWORK MADE
THE MERCEDES-BENZ 540 K ROADSTER A CLASSIC IN ITS OWN TIME, AN AUTOMOBILE WHICH DISTANCED ITSELF FROM THE ZEITGEIST
AND THE EXTRAVAGANCE WHICH CHARACTERIZED CAR BODY DESIGN IN THE LATE THIRTIES

EVER SINCE OLD TESTAMENT times, mysteries have always grown most rampantly on the soil of incomplete documentation. Although there is no such thing in our unjust world as a fair share of mystery and intrigue for all, sometimes it crops up where you would least expect – for example in the minutely regulated, smooth functioning headquarters of Mercedes-Benz.

It was almost six decades ago that the seeds of a mystery with proportions well in excess of two tons and the type number W 29 were planted at Mercedes-Benz. It is only the year of construction, 1936, which distinguishes it from the predecessor model 500 K and documents it as a member of the legendary 540 K generation. But this is far from solving the mystery, as the 540 K was constructed in no fewer than eleven bodywork versions despite being limited as a series to only 419. A search through the annals of Daimler-Benz reveals simply a mention of the black two-seater as a Sport-Roadster or Normal-Roadster. Owner Peterheinz Kern, a collector for whom lucky finds have become something of a habit, is only too pleased to quote a reference source which mentions a mere four cars of this type and offers no indication of how many could still be in existence.

Experts from the Mercedes-Benz Museum view things with somewhat more skepticism. Press officer Dieter Ritter ventures to speculate that "there could have been some more of them." And illustrated vintage car books describing this unobtrusive, somewhat conservatively styled roadster as one of the lower-powered 500 K series add still further to the confusion.

Needless to say, Peterheinz Kern is above any speculation of the kind. He knows his Mercedes vehicle identification numbers inside out. And just to be on the safe side, he actually got to work with a slide gauge in the cylinders to ascertain an 88 millimeter bore and 111 millimeter stroke – the key data for the 5401 cc of the big eight-cylinder engine. But what Kern failed to find was any trace of the prominent previous owners who could help fill in the gaps in the car's turbulent history.

After leaving the bodywork plant in Sindelfingen, the 540 K sidestepped the dubious honor of an owner from the ranks of the Nazi elite and found a home in Paris as the property of businessman Henry Gerard. Peterheinz Kern assumes that the car was first requisitioned by the German Army during World War II, and then by the US Army, as the next documented sighting was in America after the war. It was only decades later that it was sold through an English dealer back to Germany and finally fell into the hands of collector Peterheinz Kern. Judging by the condition of the car and the low mileage, it must have been more admired than driven during its life.

"It's a car without a history," comments Kern, "but for me this 540 K is just the most beautiful and most consistently styled car there is".

The elegance of this classic motor-car is reflected in cool chrome, polished like the buttons and silver braiding on the uniforms which were all the rage at the time

The plain Sindelfingen roadster lacks the extravagant flair and the flamboyance of its colleagues. Although unmistakably a product of the thirties, the front fender is styled with a far more subtle hand and does not resemble the uniform of a Field Marshall on parade. The flow of the side styling is not interrupted by two spare wheels, and the luggage compartment is like a purpose-built rucksack in comparison to the massive trunk arrangement of many of its contemporaries. The roadster from Sindelfingen was not built to transport military dignitaries, film stars and such like, but as a down-to-earth sportscar, black, elegant and made for the serious business of driving.

The austere sportscar produced in Olympic year 1936 plugs a gap in Kern's collection between two favorite collector's eras. The heart of many a collector is torn between two epochs: The heady excitement embodied by the S-Class produced in the late twenties, a combination of the Mercedes models S, SS, SSK and SSKL, the vehicles of those intrepid early pioneers of the road and racetrack, the cars in which a young Rudi Caracciola learnt supreme mastery over 300 hundred horses. The other golden age of motoring which tugs at the heartstrings of the dedicated collector is the pre-economic miracle era of the fifties, when 300 SLs, gullwings and roadsters formed the stuff of youthful dreams for the like of Heinzpeter Kern.

Even from the perspective of the darker period in German history, Kern's stance to the 540 K remains somewhat critical: "Of course, an SSKL with 7.2 liters and a supercharger of elephantine proportions runs completely differently. And the rigid axles they used make flying round corners quite a different experience than with comfortable swing axles. The 540 K is a very pleasant touring car, although I would say anything

other than a sportscar."

And as a touring car the Mercedes 540 K does look extremely tempting in the garage. The interior is decked out with opulent leather upholstery and dimensioned for cozy outings à deux. The instrument panel is designed to put across a good deal of information with a nostalgic simplicity. There is more room for luggage behind the seats than in the apology for a trunk at the back. Heinzpeter Kern and his lady were lucky enough to have the chance to travel back in time to experience this quality of travel in the vintage Monte Carlo Rally.

The sleepy, sun-drenched roads of the Westerwald area of Germany where the Mercedes 540 K has now settled into its new home are strangely reminiscent of the silent highways the Mercedes 540 K commanded during its German Reich days.

From this perspective, the Mercedes acts like a time machine which leaps sixty years into reverse at the roar of the ignition. The tiny front windshield seems to train the eye on the essentials: On the seemingly never-ending front hood with its chrome-plated hinge pointing towards that unmistakable three-pointed star, on the changing kaleidoscope of lights reflected in the polished chrome of the battery of headlamps, and on the gentle slope of the fenders. The front end of this roadster is like a landscape which can be studied when the road becomes somewhat tedious.

Not forgetting, of course, that other essential, the road. Which is important to remember when coping with the traffic of the nineties from a 1936 perspective. Job sharing is recommended under these conditions - simply shifting the what are rumored to be synchronized gears is an occupation which brooks no serious diversions. Shifting up involves skillfully coordinating the gears into synch before the teeth will engage, and shifting down is an energetic double de-clutching maneuver combined with a masterful hand on the gearstick. A fourth gear can be engaged in the form of an overdrive without fancy use of the clutch, and is activated by a carefully metered gas pedal. It is rumored that German show celebrity Marika Röck had no trouble with the transmission of her 540 K, and that the Sultan of Jahore was perfectly satisfied with the subsequently mounted normal four-speed transmission.

The Mercedes 540 K originates from an era when all self-piloted cars were met at their destination by a doorman with shiny brass buttons who whisked the car away to some mysterious parking lot. Turning the wheel at a standstill is challenge for even the most muscle-bound, and at rolling speed we encounter the indifferent light handling of an indirect worm and sector steering system, characteristically with excessive play in the central position and too little towards the end. Steering is something of a nail-biting occupation until the more experienced pilot learns to keep the car on course with a light hand. From here on in it is only a short stage to a first lesson in crass oversteering.

The new swing axle technology which was to make such an impact on chassis building was still very much in its infancy in the mid-thirties. Although this particular Mercedes actually already contained all the fundamental safety and comfort features which were to characterize the marque over the next 30 years in the form of the double control arm at the front and the double-link swing axle, roadholding technology at that time was still very much confined to the drawing board. Matters were not help-ed, either, by the size 6.00 - 16 rock-hard diagonal tires fitted onto rims which had just been widened to four inches.

But from the power unit point of view, Mercedes-Benz had done the touring car proud indeed. The all-cast iron in-line eight cylinder engine was of the simplest design with lateral camshaft and push-rod driven valves, and is an outstanding example of an engine running culture and power pure. Even by today's standards, it is a quiet engine that wields its muscle under the hood, and the casual ease with which the eight cylinders propel the car forward at less than 1000 revs merits our admiration even today.

But revs are not a subject for conversation when touring with a venerable old gentleman like the 540 K. Revs peak at around 2000, far removed from the 3400 revs per minute at which the 5.4 liter displacement produces just 115 horsepower. A spin out in the fresh spring air is more of a dignified stroll with a watchful eye on the contours of the verge than a sprightly canter. And the 180 horses which wait to spring into life at full throttle and with the roar of the supercharger are today no more than the stuff of reminiscences. "We had better not switch on the supercharger", said Heinzpeter Kern, with all the authority of someone who is not accustomed to contradiction. The thirst for driving performance is limited in any case. The driver is only too happy to reduce speed to a modest 100 km/h on country roads, while on Autobahns 130 is pushing the pilot's skills to the limits even without the added boost of the supercharger. Hats off to those early heroes who handed down yesterday's statistics: The intrepid pilots of the Daimler-Benz test driving department recorded speeds of 174 kph with a 540 K roadster. And the annals also reveal a realistic recorded acceleration time from 0 to 100 kph of 19 seconds for this 2.2 ton machine.

The intrepid drivers of the Daimler-Benz testing department took a
540 K roadster through its paces at 174 kph

THE RED OF YESTERYEAR

A HINT OF HOLLYWOOD SWEPT THROUGH THE
MERCEDES-BENZ STUDIO IN SINDELFINGEN AS STYLISTS ADDED A BOLD SWEEP TO
THE SPECIAL ROADSTER IN A BID TO EMBODY THE ZEITGEIST

AN UNEXPECTED GEM unearthed from the deepest depths of the Mercedes-Benz archives places an altogether nautical slant on the exuberant styling of this roadster. It provides an interesting demonstration on the use of the drawing board as a pointer towards a brave new future. Handed down from 1934: "The lines of the 500 K are meant to symbolize the rebirth of the German Navy. The radiator represents the stem of a ship, the fenders are the waves playing around the bows. And astern, the Mercedes demonstrates a flat rear shape reminiscent of a gunboat."

The nautical design to emerge from the distinctly non-seafaring home of Mercedes-Benz in Southern Germany in 1934 nevertheless sent out waves which swept across continents, enchanting the world with the longest fenders of all time. The luxurious expanse of sheet metal surfs effortlessly down from the front wheels, a long wavy line picked out by a bright and shiny molding. The whole effect and dimensions of the Mercedes 500 K are in total accord with the American conception of luxury: Five meters in length and a good two tons in weight, all dedicated to transporting just two people - in outstanding style, needless to say.

This somewhat disproportionate ratio and a price generally tending upwards of the basic 22,000 Reichsmarks were not without their repercussions on the sales figures. But nevertheless, 354 of the two models - the Special Roadster and the Sports Roadster - were produced between 1934 and 1936.

History has handed down this elegant car as the main protagonist in any number of antithetical scenarios. Two 500 K models won gold medals in the 2000-kilometer German Tour in 1934, for example - one of them driven by a young Rudolf Uhlenhaut 20 years before he was to turn Juan Manuel Fangio into a World Champion. King Khasi the First and the Last of Iraq also holds a place of honour in the discreetly kept list of the marque's most prominent customers. And a 500 K Coupé driven by Rudolf Caracciola appears on Daimler-Benz's list of official service cars. Not forgetting the host of beautiful women who drove a 500 K Special Roadster to victory in the one-time Concours d'Elegance, the list headed by the 1936 Cannes winner, Princess Cherwachidze.

The red Special Roadster which graces these pages spent the bloom of its youth in exile, beyond the influence of brownshirt politics. It was bought in 1936 by the Argentine "Tin King" Miguel Abreu who, despite or perhaps because of his small stature, was particularly fond of large cars. The bodywork had originally been specially designed for the princely sum of 28,000 Reichsmarks with two rows of seats one behind the other but without the box for the folding top and without the rumble seat in the luggage compartment. The four-seater fair-weather roadster reached a ripe and finally a rusty old age in South America. In 1970, the Mercedes-Benz Museum brought the car, by then little more than a wreck, and restored it as a classical roadster with two occasional seats.

In the meanwhile, this jewel of an automobile has now reached a value equivalent to an affluent mansion with its own grounds, established woodlands and all that goes with it. But it is far from being a private retreat: A red roadster of this caliber with all the youthful freshness of 58 years is far more of a presentation piece now than in it has ever been, and has long stood proud in a class of its own.

And the enjoyment of driving it has far more to do with the remarkable consistency of its styling than what it has to offer in terms of performance. In the 1936 Mercedes Roadster, the turbulence of true open-topped driving was still a standard feature of luxury class motoring. The cockpit is exposed to sun, wind and rain in more or less equal proportions: It is a kind of unspoken codex of honor that the plug-in windows remain relegated to their place in the luggage compartment and that the folding roof remains firmly tucked away – cloudbursts excepted, of course.

Only then does the windshield, a unique marriage of elegance and daring, come fully into its own. The small halves of the panes are mounted in the most delicate of chrome frames, leaving the top of the glass with no surround at all, lending this grandiose and heavy car a contrasting element of lightness. The perspective from the cockpit is like wearing rimless spectacles, and there is no other convertible which can match this open view on the world. In the distance between the star on the radiator and the firmament there is nothing but an insignificant line marking the edge

of the glass. Those were heroic days indeed, a far cry from the latter-day luxury of sunshades, roll-over resistant windscreen frames, not to mention the trusty roll-over bar.

On fine days, the roadster offers a wonderfully deep and open perspective through the windscreen. When it rains, the technology of yesteryear catches up with us in the 500 K. Minuscule windscreen wipers set up a slow and ineffectual oscillation in front of my eyes like a warning index finger enjoining me to seek refuge in the nearest garage. The message is reiterated by a few errant raindrops which climb up to the top of the windshield and fling themselves off with deadly accuracy, to land with a perverse determination exactly in my left eye.

One more endeavor on the part of an old roadster to rub off some of that polished veneer we have accumulated since those early days of motoring. Lulled into thinking we were getting along together fine at a speed of 100 km/h, the wise old roadster played its joker. Its dubious directional stability, euphemistically described all those years ago as sturdy road-holding, became more and more dubious as we went. I had that sort of sinking feeling that my venerable companion was graciously offering me the chance to pull over and deal with one of those flats our fathers used to joke about as a regular occurrence 60 years ago.

This is a way for an elderly roadster to offer a gentle reminder to a young novice about the responsibilities of the driver. After all, it is no easy matter to

Designed along the lines of modern rimless reading glasses, the windshield offers an unobstructed view on things from the star on the radiator to the firmament

wield eight cylinders and a five-liter cubic capacity with an aerodynamic drag coefficient which has the amazing capability of exercising just as great a decelerating effect as the hydraulic drum brakes which completely fill the 17 inch wheels. The earlier interpretation of what we nowadays like to call lateral acceleration on corners also calls for caution: Then it had little or nothing to do with cornering force but everything to do with the likelihood of entering into an uncontrolled spin.

The type of environment favored by the elegant Mercedes 500 K sports car is undoubtedly long straight stretches between corners. It is here that the dramatic boost of the inimitable compressor - which gave it the K (Kompressor) in its name - comes fully into play.

Normally speaking, this gigantic piece of engineering wizardry, which boasts a full one meter stretch between cylinders one and eight and a total cast iron mass of 600 kilos, is placid enough with its 100 horses kept decently in check. But a determined tread on the gas pedal unleashes a completely different side to its nature, the supercharger screeching like the proverbial banshee as it whips 160 horses up to 1200 rpm under boost pressure. What really places the sensation far beyond that experienced in a well-oiled diesel engine, though, is that unearthly wail of the supercharger, so intoxicating and habit-forming that it ought by rights to be banned. One American connoisseur defined that inimitable sound as the definitive "war cry of the Valkyrie".

60 years ago,
factual efficiency at
Mercedes-Benz was
expressed in a blend
of cream and chrome

ENTER THE EMPEROR

A TURNING CIRCLE OF FOURTEEN METERS. BUT HARDLY EVER PUT TO USE

THERE WERE TWO HOURS to go before the return of the Emperor, but the sidewalks were slowly filling. School gates swung open to release a flow of children, who formed neat ranks along the sides of the road, each small hand clutching a flag. Adults searched out prime positions, but despite the possibility of a bird's-eye view, not a single head appeared at any of the upper floor windows. An age-old but still respected taboo prohibits anyone from looking down upon the Emperor.

At brief intervals, Police loudspeakers boomed out bulletins of the Emperor's progress and the latest estimates of his expected time of arrival in Okitsu. Police jeeps periodically swept along the street, every time triggering off a premature sea of waving flags. The entire town had been cordoned off to traffic.

A passing megaphone truck announced: "The Emperor has now entered Okitsu." A few suspect raindrops failed to deter the waiting masses, which seemed to stretch as one body to peer towards the end of the road. The general murmur of conversation rose to an excited babble, a furious brandishing of flags set up. At last the first two machines of the police motorcade were spotted, driving just fast enough for them to stay upright.

And then it appeared, the majestic Mercedes-Benz, an automobile fit for an Emperor and with an Emperor's disdain for fads and fashions. Its angular black roof rose proud above the subservient, cowed limousines which crept along behind, its body powerful, magnificent. It bore the golden chrysanthemum along its flank."

This is how Oliver Statler described the Emperor's visit to Minaguchi-ya, the strangely legendary resting place between Tokyo and the ancient royal residence of Kyoto. Especially appealing is his reference to the royal "disdain for fads and fashions": This event took place in 1957, after all, when the big Mercedes had already passed its twentieth birthday. And probably looked even older with its Pullman limousine superstructure, a feature which was already considered - shall we say - conservative back in the thirties. The Emperor liked to show off his royal personage in this car right through into the sixties, even though the royal fleet contained more than its fair share of modern Rolls and Daimlers.

In this strict and archaic form, the Big Mercedes had little in common with those last powerfully elegant and usually open-topped models which conveyed the Nazi elite. From 1930 to 1945, the series continued to be called the Type 770, or the "Big Mercedes" to most, despite underlying technical modernization in 1938 and a gradual but unmistakable bodywork transformation over the years - all hand crafted and with a scrutinizing eye to every individual requirement.

The Japanese Royal Household ordered seven of these splendid specimens between 1932 and 1935. One was destroyed during an air raid

The dignitaries lowered themselves onto a cover of the finest fabric, the poor chauffeur had to make do with leather. A signalling device kept him posted of wishes from on high

An engine fit for a King under the hood: The 7.7 liter eight-cylinder produced 150 bhp (without booster) at as low as 2800 rpm

Space at a premium: The Pullman superstructure was far more perpendicular in its styling than other bodywork variations produced for the Big Mercedes during its first years. Kings and Emperors could preserve their dignity but still feel they were "on the road"

in the war, three were held back "in reserve" (as noble spare parts carriers, perhaps?) and three continued in active duty up to modern times. The model shown here found its way back to Untertürkheim in 1971, where it now resides in the Mercedes-Benz Museum.

The 7.7-litre in-line eight-cylinder engine whose magnificent torque would lead the uninitiated to expect a far more royal performance than the meager 150 bhp at 2800 revs (with the additional boost of the supercharger it mustered 200 horses - but who could envisage a turbo-propelled Emperor of Japan?).

Hirohito was absolutely the most discreet Mercedes-driven dignitary imaginable. Kaiser Wilhelm II while in exile in Holland had his magnificent marine-gray model kitted out with what amounted to ship's telegraph communication system between the quarter deck and the helm, involving a complex system of signals. The Emperor of Japan made his wishes known to his chauffeur in more modest style, using an indicator with the commands: Start, slow, stop, left, right, back to the palace.

THE COURSE OF TRUE LOVE

THIS IS THE STORY OF THE WORLD'S GREATEST LIVING ENTHUSIAST AND HIS LOVE FOR
A GENERATION OF CARS WHICH NECESSARILY PLAYED A ROLE IN THE POWER DEMONSTRATIONS OF THE NAZIS.
BUT TRUE LOVE IS ABOVE ALL SUSPICION

JAN MELIN has the advantage of coming from neutral Sweden, a fact which was never of greater value than during the years of his early childhood. Jan, born in 1937, grew up in Uppsala the son of a research scientist who had traveled the uncharted reaches of the Amazon back in the twenties.

In 1949, when Jan was twelve, a friend telephoned to spread the news that his father had bought a super car. Jan lost no time in racing over to his friend's house, only five minutes away, to survey the new acquisition: A breathtakingly beautiful dark blue car with its roof folded down, traces of the Swedish royal coat of arms still visible on the doors.

It was a Mercedes-Benz 320 dating from 1938 which had belonged to Prince Gustaf Adolf, the father of the present King. The Prince, who was to have become King in his turn, was killed in an air crash in 1947.

It was all of 45 years ago that a young and impressionable lad stood and stared at a dark blue car which seemed to hold him entranced. It was a first taste of a world he was anxious to find out more about.

At first, the closest he was able to get to gleaning information was to study the daily papers for advertisements. It was a buyer's market for large Mercedes models in those early post-war days: Times were hard and petrol was at a premium. He went to Stockholm and saw his first supercharged car in the showroom of a Mercedes importer. Enthralled, he collected all the documentation he could lay his hands on.

He began his studies in electronics engineering in Gothenburg and his collection continued to swell. In the meanwhile he had narrowed down his field of special interest to the supercharged Mercedes models produced during the thirties. Gradually, the more powerful eight-cylinder models began to take the upper hand in his affections against the sportier six-cylinders of the twenties.

He began to correspond with the Mercedes plant, to meet like minded people. He got married and even maneuvered his honeymoon to take in Stuttgart. Those early nights of nuptial bliss hold a very special memory for Melin: Him on his knees, she on her knees, he would say a number, she would answer tenderly with another number and he wrote down the figures in consecutive sequence, creating a comprehensive index of supercharged models which could later be matched up to the right body. The result was a complete identity for the each overall car, all in consecutive sequence - something which could previously only be put together in the works archive as a result of leafing backwards and forwards through endless records, a process in which one piece could be twenty volumes distant from the next.

It should not be omitted to mention that during those years of elementary research, Jan Melin found the leisure to produce two beautiful daughters, to finance his course of study by performing as a jazz pianist,

and to launch a successful career as a communications electronics engineer. Not that anyone should form a picture of the man as some sort of obsessive crackpot. Nothing could be further from the truth. Jan Melin is a man with the enviable talent of loving people as well as things, and he possesses greater love and patience than most would imagine.

In the mid-sixties he worked as an electronics engineer in the USA, taking this opportunity to work his way through the American archives, burrowing ever deeper into the available material. To him, material now meant first and foremost documentation and data on the eight-cylinder supercharger models produced from 1930 onwards into the war years, the 380, 500 K, 540 K and of course the type 770, the Big Mercedes.

The aspect which most fascinated him were bodywork details, those fine differences which were discernible practically in every model which hailed from those pre-mass-production days. He tried to trace the thinking behind those special touches added by the coachmakers, and somehow managed to form a contact with Hermann Ahrens, the most important coachwork specialist in the thirties. Melin was bursting with a thousand questions, screened Ahrens's private archive down to the very last drop of information, taxed his memory to reach into the darkest corners of his memory. He rummaged through all the drafts and drawings he could lay hands on in Sindelfingen, entangled himself in the many hundreds of ancillary drawings, the products of widely varying imaginations, ideas, put into practice or simply sketched out - every last scrap of information comes alive to he who knows how to interpret it.

Certain fundamental styling elements he found particularly stimulating: The radiator positioned slightly behind the front axle during some years, the long hood, the proudly undulating fenders which lent a sweeping majesty to the side view, and that perfect finishing touch, the pointed radiator!

By the mid eighties, Melin had come to a point where he felt he could no longer simply absorb more information without presenting some of what he had discovered and gathered to the world at large. So all the decades of collecting, of burrowing, of research found their way into a book entitled: "Mercedes Benz. The Supercharged 8-Cylinder Cars of the 1930s". The result was a sensation in terms of accuracy and completeness of material, including no fewer than six hundred photographs from the thirties! It represented the culmination of a total of 36 trips to Stuttgart, but it was an effort which was worth the making. At long last, here was a reference work, a mine of information for other like-minded enthusiasts. The publication brought forth a flood of enthusiastic response, with no fewer than 600 letters from all over the world and ecstatic reviews in specialized journals. The fact that he never saw a single penny for his pains must be put down to experience - the publishing house happened to go bankrupt before the author received his first check.

Be that as it may, Melin is still nothing but thankful: After all, the publishers had brought the book to the public eye, his work was available in five thousand copies with enough information to quench even the most thirsty. And after all, he had never cherished a desire to make money from his love of old cars. Even the tremendous amount he had spent in the gathering of his material took on an almost sacrificial significance once he knew that he would never recoup it.

And anyone expressing the view that this dry browsing though endless archives cannot possibly have been enjoyable is entitled to his own opinion, of course. Undeniably this was a very special love affair. But simply the joy of writing what you know yourself for definite to be absolutely the truth, one hundred per cent accurate, each number, each figure - that is the essence of pleasure to a man of Melin's caliber. He has no patience with superficial flick-of-the-wrist journalism which cares not one whit where its material comes from. That this particular school does not even take the trouble to check its facts against his reference work is something which can ruffle his otherwise placid nature.

The book has also brought him happiness in other ways, as it has been a means of opening up contacts to other people and cars. He has been approached by other enthusiasts, and had the chance to take the wheel of some of his beloved automobile classics himself. It is a sad irony that the greatest enthusiast of them all has never found his way to ownership of one of the objects of his passion - not even one of the smallest. In the fifties, when they could be picked up cheaply, he was a student, and to-day's prices are simply beyond his reach. But Jan Melin him-self bears no grudges, calling himself "Only an enthusiast, not an owner". This is not something which should be considered a point of principle: A tidy gift from an oil sheikh did not go unappreciated.

The 500 K and 540 K Special Roadster and Coupé dated 1936 and 1937 are the epitome of automotive elegance for Melin. He considers the period from 1934 to 1937 generally to have been the heyday of car body design, save for the later 770 models. The 770, called the Big Mercedes, is a chapter unto itself. It is a car whose showmanship qualities capture him in quite a different way. Just to see such a 770! Or even to drive one! Incredible!

During the seventies, he had the opportunity to look at the car driven by King Haakon of Norway. He sat in front of it for three hours without moving - like a devoted art student in front of a painting. Yes, Melin confirms: "The feeling you get is the same as you experience looking at a painting - some it grips with an intensity which defies description, some it leaves completely cold."

The designation 770 or Big Mercedes remained unaltered between 1930 and 1944, but 1938 saw a fundamental change in the design, when the chassis was altered to the W 150.

Melin decidedly opts for the later version. It was more mature from the technical point of view, and its body structures were more elegant, although this preference does expose him more than ever to the question of possible conflict between innocent enthusiasm for an automobile and the associations the car necessarily awakens with the Nazi elite. Despite the fact that there were many ordinary business people who drove a 770, even in neutral Sweden, there is something which binds this model inextricably to the show of power which was part and parcel of the Nazi regime. Is it possible for Melin to separate politics completely from the object of his life-long passion?

Melin's response: "I may be extremely naive, but the simple truth is that I am interested purely and simply in the cars as cars. When I battled my way through 300,000 photos in the Washington archives which the Americans had from the Germans, they were amazed: Of the people who had come to browse though the records in search of material for historical research, I was the only one truly and absolutely interested in just the cars. Of course many of the photos contain Nazi statues and what have you - but I pay these practically no attention. Neither does it affect me at all who happens to be sitting in the car at the time. Of course I am aware that other observers react quite differently. But it would be unthinkable and indeed ridiculous to attempt to pass over this whole era as if it had never happened. Books actually exist which stop with the six-cylinder models of the early thirties and carry on with the 170. What happened, happened: In terms of automotive engineering development, the thirties were the golden era for Mercedes. That is the fact and no amount of turning the blind eye will make it go away."

Over the years, though, Melin has been stripped of a good deal of his naiveté. True love is rare, business sense less so. Because in our day and age a Big Mercedes is likely to fetch a higher price if it can be linked to one of the infamous Nazi names (best of all naturally the "Führer's car"), caution is called for. At the request of the manufacturer, Melin does not answer inquiries relating to chassis or other numbers, as they fear that the result could be another shiny Göring service car to rise phoenix-like from the scrap heap. Melin has no indication that a true Nazi car enthusiast scene really exists, but like in any walk of life: The more famous (or infamous) the previous history, the higher the asking price.

The 770 was offered with a range of different bodies, and the reader will be correct in assuming that Jan Melin has collected and described all there is to be known about them. He personally prefers the open models which he considers to show off the styling and reveal the integral beauty of the whole to best advantage. The single most important element he considers to be the radiator, the car's enormous V-nosed crowning glory with its enormous Bosch headlamps, and the two whole meters of nothing but engine hood. We now know that the cars transporting the Führer himself were fitted with an additional pedestal mounted on small plateau under the folded-down seat - lending him the advantage of a couple more inches.

There was a curious incongruity between the exposure up above and the customary all-round armored protection on the sides and underneath, which included a retractable armored plate at the back and windows which could be as thick as 40 mm - in which case 400 turns of the crank were needed to raise them to their full height. An open-topped armored touring car of the 770 (W 150) series was six meters in length, weighed up to 4,230 kg, and had a permissible payload of just 500 kilos. The maximum horsepower, 230 bhp with supercharger from 7.7 liters, could only be utilized up to a speed of 80 kph before – understandably – initiating a tire alarm. The quick accelerating non-armored version served up a top speed of as high as 170 kph – what a feeling!

Despite its additional burden, Melin claims, maneuverability was surprisingly good - apart from squeezing into parking spaces, which this type of car clearly rarely had to do. Brakes so-so, driving characteristics flawless, even if it is difficult to imagine how they made it up to Obersalzberg in snowy and icy conditions.

Melin's very favorite automobile children are those with a Scandinavian connection - and there are certainly some splendid specimens to be found. If forced to opt for one absolute out-and-out favorite, says Melin: It would have to be the Mannerheim car.

Carl Gustaf Mannerheim is Finland's best-known personality of the century. He already had an eventful military and political career behind him when he led his country into the Winter War of 1939/40 against the Soviet Union and attempted to attempt to regain the territory lost in the process during the "Follow-on war" (1941 to 44) by Germany's side. Mannerheim pursued his own highly individual Finnish policy and had little time for the Nazis. All that connected them was their common foe. In 1941, Hitler presented Field Marshall Mannerheim with a Big Mercedes, the "Open touring car" version, the single most spectacular

The recipient loved the gift, but not the giver:
Marshal Gustav Mannerheim on a tour of inspection during the war in
Finland. The Big Mercedes was a personal "token" from Hitler to Finland's
commander in chief

version of the 770. The car was dark blue, armored of course. It weighed 4100 kg, was 5980 mm long, 2050 mm wide, and stood 1800 mm high with the folding roof closed. The car was first driven to Hitler's Headquarters in East Prussia where it was inspected by Hitler himself, and then shipped to Finland and presented to Mannerheim. Hitler's own chauffeur Erich Kempka was sent to train Mannerheim's chauffeur Kauko Ranta.

Six months later, on Mannerheim's 75th birthday, Hitler turned up after only a few hours' warning to congratulate the Field Marshal in person. He was flown into Immola in a Focke-Wulf 200, picked up in the Mercedes and taken to the Finnish leader's special train. He flew back only a couple of hours later.

Mannerheim seems to have been extremely fond of the car, if not of its donor. Jan Melin, who – not unexpectely – later spoke with Mannerheim's chauffeur, knows about the Marshall's predilection for fast driving, about the difficulties involved in keeping the wide wheel base on track on gravel or snow-covered roads, and about the washing ritual which took four hours. He is privy to the special petrol stores (German gas was needed as the Finnish variety was not of a high enough octane), and is informed about the moderate consumption of only 27 liters to 100 kilometers. And he knows, too, that a set of snow chains lasted around 400 km, the heating was sufficient even at -20 degrees, and that four hot air channels kept the windscreen free of ice at all times. He is familiar with the leather cases kept for spares, one of the electrics, one for the engine, and the fact that they were lined with velvet. A leather bag with silver hardware contained 64 medicinal articles, all labeled both in German and Finnish, ranging from headache powder to remedies to be employed in case of gassing. Even the chauffeur had his own bag containing a clothes

Heikki Jaakola

The Mannerheim car in all its splendour, photographed in the summer of 1942 in front of the Marshall's headquarters in Mikkeli.
The number plate refutes any Nazi connection: This is the personal vehicle of the commander in chief of the Finnish Army (Suomen Armeja)

Nils Johansson

brush and shaving apparatus, including a lather brush and mirror.

In 1944, Finland made its peace with the Soviet Union, and Mannerheim was made State President. The car had served its time, had now become something of a political embarrassment, and in 1947 was sent to Sweden to be sold. Taking pride of place in the showroom of a big Mercedes dealer in Stockholm, it attracted a huge crowd of on-lookers. A brewery owner from the provinces who was just driving past in his 540 K wondered what all the fuss was about. When he found out, he left his own car there, agreed to pay the difference, and drove on with the Field Marshall's Big Mercedes home to his loved ones in Eskilstuna. The family could only stand and stare in awe, as indeed did the whole village. As the Mannerheim car was not the most practical mode of transport for making local purchases (so many crowds gathering round in front of the shops!), the family urged him to sell. During those postwar days of exchange rate compensation a deal involving ball bearings between General Motors and Sweden eventually brought the Big Mercedes after a number of twists and turns into the hands of a private owner in Chicago. Before it came to its final resting place, though, the arrival of the historical vehicle in New York's harbor was celebrated with true American enthusiasm, the car was exhibited in the Rockefeller Center before being used for charity tours. The car with the chassis number 429317 turned up at an auction in the mid seventies in Scottsdale, where it was grandly if somewhat inaccurately presented as the "Führer's car", producing goose bumps of delighted horror among the auction-goers. The car found its way to California, again to a private owner, and it is currently in the throes of being restored. Jan Melin's face lights up: "Such a beautiful car! You should take a long look at the radiator – such a beauty, so big – and that unmistakable V-nose!"

LIGHTFOOT WITH 750 KILOS

THE HEYDAY OF THE SILVER ARROW BEGAN
WHEN DESIGNERS WERE FORCED TO THINK LIGHT:
THE W125 IS A MASTERPIECE OF ENGINEERING CRAFTSMANSHIP

FOLLOWING WORLD WAR I, the Grand Prix racing circuit was overwhelmingly in the hands of the French, Italian, and partly also the British marques. These were the eras of the three-liter formula (1920/21), the two-liter formula (1922 to 1925) and the 1.5-liter formula (1926/1927). During the years that followed, Grand Prix races were generally held freestyle. The twenties were characterized, too, by magnificent performances from Ballot, Delage, Fiat, Sunbeam and Bugatti; Mercedes had yet to bring out a really successful Grand Prix model. This was changed with the introduction of the 750 formula, which remained in effect until 1937.

The 750 kg Formula was brought into being in 1932 by the former Alliance Internationale des Automobile Clubs Reconnus (AIACR), predecessor to the FIA. During the twenties, racing Formulas were defined predominantly on the basis of displacement limitation. By defining a maximum weight, the intention was to keep overpowered monster machines off the racetracks. This was not to be, as producers, particularly Mercedes-Benz and Auto Union, found a way of constructing relatively large-volumed racing cars with highly powerful engines using extreme lightweight construction methods. The first W25 with supercharged eight-cylinder engine had a capacity of 3.36 liters. Over the course of the following three racing seasons, the Grand Prix machine was gradually injected with increasing capacity: first to 3.72, then 3.99, 4.3 and 4.74 liters. The result was a gradual increase in output from the original 302 bhp of the M25 engine at the start of 1934 up to the grand 456 bhp achieved from the big 4.74-litre ME25 engine in 1936.

The 1934 W25 racing car achieved four Grand Prix victories in the face of tough opposition from Auto Union with its successful V16 engine. In 1935, the upgraded eight-cylinder experienced a record season, clocking up no fewer than 9 victories over 11 races. The euphoria of the 1935 season stood out in stark contrast to the disappointments of the following year: In 1936 Rudolf Caracciola managed to notch up only the Monaco and Tunis Grand Prix races following a whole series of technical hitches with the 4.7 liter ME 25 engine, which kept Mercedes-Benz from even attending some of the Grand Prix venues during that troubled year. 1936 marked a triumphant year for Auto Union and its beaming 27-year-old talent Bernd Rosemeyer. Its rear-engine (today we would refer to it as a mid-engine) swept the car from one victory to the next, its success shining all the brighter for the miserable plight of the Mercedes team.

Setting its sights on 1937, a disillusioned racing department at Untertürkheim decided to sweep the board and design a completely new racing car. The newly formed racing department was attached to the development and testing department under the management of Fritz Nallinger, and the young engineer Rudolf Uhlenhaut was put in overall charge of racing technology.

The Mercedes-Benz W125 built in 1937 was celebrated (alongside the Auto Union Type C) as the most striking and outstanding racing car of the 750 kg Grand Prix formula applicable from 1934 to 1937. The mighty supercharged eight-cylinder engine with its cubic capacity of 5,660 cc produced up to 600 bhp, while supplying a sensational power-to-weight ratio of around 1.25 kg/bhp

The new racing car was given the type designation W125, and was based on a tubular frame comprising oval tubes in chrome-nickel molybdenum steel with a wall thickness of 1.5 mm. The frame weighed 52 kg, the wheel base was 2794 mm.

The construction of the eight-cylinder in-line engine designed by Albert Ress demonstrated the same basic features used by Mercedes-Benz since 1914: The engine block was formed not of a single cast component, but a welded steel construction, and each cylinder had its own welded-on water jacket. In comparison to the power packs used between 1934 and 1936, the cylinder spacing had been slightly increased, making the engine somewhat longer overall. The cylinder dimensions were 94 mm for the bore and 102 mm for the stroke, generating a cubic capacity of 5660 cc. The crankshaft, which incidentally did not come from Hirth, was mounted in nine bearings instead of the five used in the previous racing engine. The dual camshaft machine had four sodium-filled valves per cylinder. The valves were 39 mm in diameter, and created an angle of 70° between them. Originally, the 223 kg engine was compressed to 8.9:1, later 9.4:1. Another interesting development was the move away from the conventional method of feeding compressed air to the carburetors during charging with the vertically positioned Roots supercharger in favor of pressing the mixture from the carburetors into the combustion chamber by means of a induction supercharger. The engine operated at a boost pressure of 0.65 at. The connecting rods were given an H-shaped cross-section, and the forged light metal pistons from Mahle weighed 500 g a piece.

During the 1937 season, Mercedes-Benz drove with a fuel mixture comprising 86.0% methyl alcohol, 8.8% acetone, 4.4% nitrobenzene and 0.8% ether. The high proportion of methyl alcohol was necessary in order to cool the engine from the inside. The racing fuels used in those days were caustic, and excessive periods spent chasing the tail of an adversary cannot have done the pilots any good. With its W125, Mercedes-Benz launched the use of the modern chassis construction method which was to be retained by most designers practically up until the end of the fifties, when there was a general change in favor of the mid-engine construction. The W125 was the first prominent Grand Prix car to sport the De-Dion rear axle: The De-Dion principle had been known since the beginning of the century, although most racing designers stuck with the rigid rear axle until right into thirties. In the new Mercedes racing model, the De-Dion axle comprised a screw-mounted element, with the short central section acting as a type of joint. It worked through the sliding movement of a hardened steel ball in a vertical slot on the rear end of the gear/differential box, which guaranteed the lateral guidance of the entire rear axle construction. The two drive shafts were jointed inside and out. The De-Dion construction was guided on the longitudinal side by two flat, perforated longitudinal control arms which were controlled at the two main tubes of the tubular frame on a level with the steering wheel. At the back, suspension was effected by means of torsion bars. The hydraulic shock absorbers were mounted at the back-most chassis cross members, with their arms running parallel to the drive shafts. The gearbox, located behind the driver and forming a unit with the differential, had only four speeds. The front wheel suspension comprised wishbones located one above the other, each connected to a helical spring. Here, too, the shock absorbers were hydraulic.

The eight-cylinder in-line engine and power transmission were located on a plane which dropped slightly towards the back, permitting the

driver to sit somewhat lower than usual. The long wheelbase and the weight concentration of the car at the front as a result of the front-mounted engine, and back due to the position of the gearbox/differential, made the car highly stable on the straight. In corners, the W125 was said to understeer, but a slight touch on the gas pedal allowed the pilot to easily force a spin of the large wheels with their relatively narrow tread, and so steer the car on course.

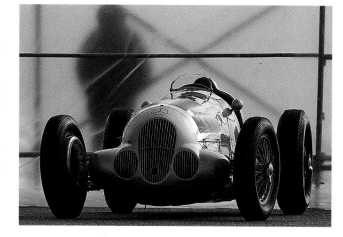

With the overall transmission ratio as it was used on medium-speed racetracks, the Grand Prix car achieved 120 kph at 5500 rpm in first, 185 in second, 215 in third and 270 kph in top gear. The corresponding statis-tics for the ratio to be used at Monza were 141, 219, 254 and 318 kph. During the Belgian Grand Prix, a top speed of 310.34 kph was registered in the W 125 on the very fast but in some cases also bumpy road combinations of Spa-Francorchamps.

The very first of the new 5.6 liter monopostos designed for the 1937 Grand Prix season was ready by February of that year for initial performance testing. The elegantly styled body was made of aluminum paneling and weighed 30.5 kg. The drag coefficient of 0.59 was relatively good for a racing car with free-standing wheels.

The W125 was piloted by Rudolf Caracciola, then 37, a familiar face in the Mercedes team with the 1935 European Championship to his name, and also Manfred Brauchitsch, already a member of the Mercedes-Benz team for a number of years. Brauchitsch seemed to be the eternal victim of technical gremlins, which had left him with a reputation for being un-

lucky. The former side-car passenger Hermann Lang, then 28, was given a place in the Grand Prix team in 1935 after working as a mechanic for Mercedes-Benz in 1934 with responsibility for the car driven by Italian Luigi Fagioli. Lang had not won any previous car races. In 1937 the Englishman Richard Seaman, then only 24, was taken on as a new member of the Grand Prix team. Seaman had excelled himself over a period of several years as a Voiturette pilot (1.5-litre supercharged racing cars) for MG, Delage and ERA, and was considered an outstanding talent. A young Swiss pilot by the name of Christian Kautz, 24 years of age, also joined the prestigious German racing team under contract. He had achiev-ed a string of successes for Bugatti and Maserati in the Voiturette category and was also considered highly promising.

The wind-up of the 1937 season also saw the end of the 750 kg racing formula, which had in fact achieved the opposite of what the regulating bodies had intended, in other words to restrict engine output and so reduce top speeds. Due to the implementation of modern engineering and chassis construction techniques, but in particular as a result of consistent and elaborate lightweight construction methods, the German marques dominated practically right across the board during the four consecutive seasons from 1934 to 1937, with the Mercedes W125 and also the Auto Union Type 0 taking pride of place in the annals of racing history as the most outstanding representatives of the age.

THE TRIPOLI VICTORY

ONCE RACED, NEVER FORGOTTEN:
THE BRIEF BUT HEADLONG CAREER OF THE SMALL MERCEDES WITH THE LION HEART

THE OUTBREAK OF WAR put a premature end to the Grand Prix career of the W 165, the "small" Mercedes-Benz racing car, after only a single race. However, that one race, the 1939 Tripoli Grand Prix, saw a much-applauded victory in the 1.5 liter Voiturette category which at the time was firmly in the grip of the Italian marques. The W 165 was Mercedes-Benz's first V8 engine design.

The Mercedes racing engineers had built the car under cover of secrecy within the incredibly short period of just under eight months following the surprise announcement that there would be a Tripoli Grand Prix contested for the Voiturette category. The political events of 1939 meant that the W165 was never to race again. After the war, work did continue on a further development of the "Tripoli Car" up to 1951, until in the autumn of that year a decision was finally taken to pursue a different course following a resolution by the International Sports Committee to open the Driver's World Championship in 1952 and 1953 to Formula Two racing cars with two-liter induction engines.

The three-liter supercharged formula introduced in 1938 (cars with a 4.5 liter induction engine were also permitted to join) was entirely dominated by the Mercedes-Benz and Auto Union racing models. The only other manufacturers building cars with any remote chance of competing were Alfa Romeo and Maserati. In September 1938, during the Grand Prix meeting in Italy in 1939, word went round that all Grand Prix races on

Italian territory in 1939 would only be open to 1.5 liter racing cars of the Voiturette category, as the Italian marques were the dominating force in this field. During the middle of the 1938 season the new Alfa Romeo 158 "Alfetta" appeared for the first time, and looking ahead to 1939, Maserati worked on its new 4CM model with four valves per cylinder following a successful string of victories for the Maserati 4CM 1500 or 6CM. At that time, Libya was an Italian colony, with the result that the supercharged 1.5 liter racing car category was stipulated for the North African Grand Prix too. Just a few days after the Italian Grand Prix race on September 15, 1938, a meeting took place in Untertürkheim, when interest was clearly expressed in the construction of a 1.5 liter monoposto. On November 18, 1938, the General Management gave the go-ahead for the design, and by mid-February, 1939, the entire folder of design drawings was ready. Three type W165 chassis were built, as well as three type W154 engines with the supercharged V12 three-liter engine which had played such a dominating role in the 1938 championship season and which underwent further development in anticipation of 1939 to become the W154/M163. A shortened W154 chassis was used with a wheel base reduced to 2,540 mm. The track width was 1.340 mm at the front and 1.280 mm at the back. Once again, the chassis was based on the classical oval tubular construction made of chrome nickel molybdenum steel. And on this occasion, too, the engine and transmission were installed in a sloping arrangement

offset by 6°, as in the W154, with the driver's seat offset slightly to the right. In the slightly asymmetrical vehicle interior, the driver was able to sit on the right next to the drive shaft, permitting a lower driving position. The tubular frame with the two large longitudinal members was defined by the Mercedes engineers as the most torsion-resistant chassis to have emerged to date from the Mercedes workshops.

The engine represented new country to the developers, as a decision was taken in favor of a V8. The 8-cylinder was also built using a typical Mercedes-Benz construction with cylinder assemblies welded onto steel plates and encircled by a steel jacket (for circulation of the coolant glycol, which has an extremely high boiling point), which as a block formed a fork angle of 90°. The forged chrome nickel steel crankshaft was mounted in five main roller bearings, each of which activated two pairs of camshafts, each with four valves per cylinder (mercury-cooled outlet valves). These formed an angle of 56°. The cylinder dimensions were 64 x 58 mm = 1,495 cc, the compression ratio 7:1. The power unit was still supercharged by two parallel operating roots compressors; the two-stage blower which was installed in the 1939 three-liter V12 engine was planned for a later development stage of the M165. The compressors generated a boost pressure of 1.4 at. The forged Mahle pistons were fitted once again with two sealing rings and two oil stripping rings. The oil circulation encompassed 14 liters. Two Solex horizontal carburetors took care of gas mixture preparation. During its first test stand trials, the V8 generated 256 bhp at 8,000 revs. The revolutions were then restricted to 7,500 rpm, corresponding to 245 bhp to be sure of complying with the regulations. The 190 kg eight-cylinder power pack was thus more powerful than the eight-cylinder in-line engine used in the Alfa Romeo 158 which produced 225 bhp at 7,500 rpm at that time. In order to ensure that the handling characteristics were as neutral as possible, the W165 was fitted with a large central tank between the pilot and the engine as well as a relatively small rear tank which did not quite fill out the space below the body as it tapered towards the back. In total, the car was capable of carrying 245 liters of fuel, most of which was taken from the central tank. With its tanks empty, the W165 weighed 718 kg, with a full fuel load 905 kg, with 53.3% of the weight resting on the rear axle.

The W165 achieved the following top speeds at 7.500 rpm in the five gears: 90 in first, 155 in second, 184 in third 234 in fourth and 272 in fifth. Although a production order for three chassis and three engines had been approved, finally only two complete cars were built.

Initial test driving took place on April 7th at 7 in the morning at Hockenheim: Rudolf Caracciola and Hermann Lang together covered around 500 km practically without a hitch. There was not much time to go before the car's public debut on May 7th, and on May 4th the W165 arrived for its first training session in Tripoli. While the previous season's top qualifying time for a 1.5 liter racing car had been over four minutes, Lang with his longer transmission ratio notched up a time of 3:45.7; Caracciola's fast-est round was completed in 3:52.7. The next day, the two Mercedes were beaten by a new Maserati 4CL with streamlined bodywork driven by Luigi Villoresi, who set a new lap time record of 3:41.8 = 211.7 kph. This placed the Italian in pole position. Lang improved his time to 3:42.3.

In keeping with tradition, Marshall Italo Balbo gave the starting signal for the 30 lap race with the Tricolore, but all the pilots had been instructed to go by the starting traffic light, which actually switched a split

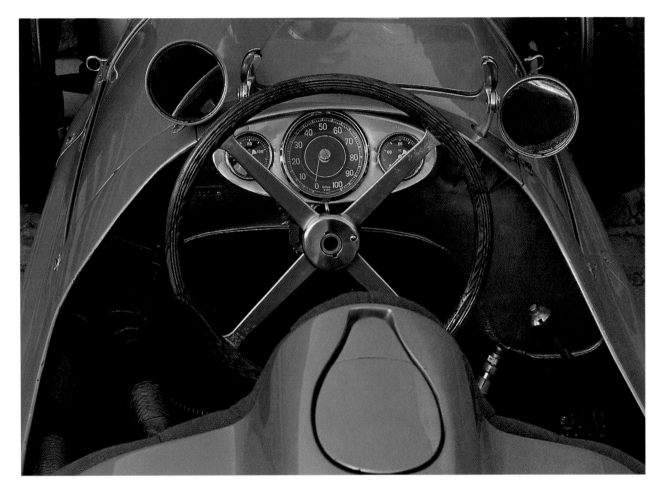

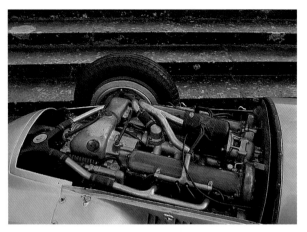

In the 1.5-liter V8-engined W165, too,
the power unit was mounted at an incline to allow
the driver to sit next to the power train.
This meant a slightly asymmetrical cockpit.
The power unit was the first V8 construction
to emerge from Untertürkheim,
supercharged by dual Roots blowers

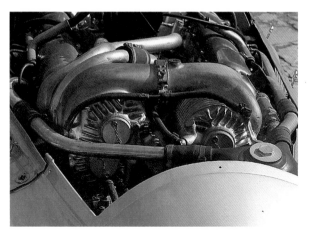

second beforehand. Lang reacted to the signal and in so doing gained an initial advantage over the rest of the field. Training record holder Luigi Villoresi yielded his pole position with transmission problems right from the beginning, and was forced to retire after only a single lap. Lang succeeded in shaking off his rivals straight away, and Guiseppe Farina in the Alfa Romeo 158 gained a lead over Caracciola's Mercedes, only to drop out later in the race. Lang drew in for refueling and tire change with a considerable lead. The speedy south German pilot, who had joined the Mercedes racing department as a mechanic and worked on Luigi Fagioli's car in 1934, won the Tripoli Grand Prix with almost a lap in hand before team-mate Caracciola. Lang covered the 393 km course with an average speed of 197.8 km/h, and he also drove the fastest lap in 3:43.7 = 211.6 km/h in lap 12. The double victory scored by the Mercedes W165 in its maiden Grand Prix venue went down in the annals of motor racing history: A car put on the tarmac in just under eight months had managed to achieve the unthinkable: to beat the Italians whose specialized skills were concentrated on the 1.5 liter category. This was to be the W 165's first and last competitive appearance, although two weeks after the triumph in Tripoli, the two North Africa heroes drove a lap of honor on the Nürburgring. Despite the outbreak of war, work went on in Untertürkheim on the W165 with a view to the 1940 Tripoli Grand Prix (the race actually took place and ended with a victory for the Alfetta). The order had actually been given for the construction of a fourth chassis and a fourth and fifth engine on January 29, 1940, but the final whistle was blown for the W165 on March 26th. Further developments and chassis improvements had already been carried out on one of the cars, a larger rear tank was mounted and work on the two-stage blower had also progressed considerably. An output of 278 horsepower was registered on the test stand at 8,250 rpm.

Together with all the rest of the Mercedes racing hardware, the W165 was kept in hiding near Dresden during the war. When the war was over, Rudolf Caracciola, who was living in Switzerland, attempted to convey the two Mercedes W165s over the border in a truck, but they were confiscated at the Swiss border. But by April 1946, Caracciola had achieved his goal. After his personal mechanic Walz had managed to bring one of the cars to life, Caracciola completed a test drive on a disused road near Schlieren near Zurich. But the car's racing days were definitely over, and the two models were auctioned in 1950, the highest bid coming from Mercedes-Benz Switzerland.

By this time, Mercedes-Benz had so far emerged from the difficulties of the immediate post-war period to be feeling the Grand Prix itch once again. On June 15, 1951, the General Management ordered the construction of five new W165s for Formula One participation.

After the German Grand Prix on July 29, which was won by Alberto Ascari in a Ferrari 375 with 4.5 liter induction engine, Rudolf Caracciola and Mercedes test pilot Karl Kling drove a few test laps on the Nürburgring with the W165, which had by this time returned home to the fold. Although work had progressed well on the engines, which were now in tiptop condition, the times achieved on the Nürburgring were not particularly encouraging. Added to this, the International Sport Commission passed a resolution in October 1951 to run the Driver's World Championships in 1952 and 1953 with Formula Two racing cars (two-liter induction engines), leaving the Mercedes-Benz 1.5 liter supercharger project without a sensible objective.

TWELVE-CYLINDER MAGIC

A RARE BREED: THE GRAND PRIX WINNERS OF THE LATE THIRTIES
CONCEALED BRUTE POWER BENEATH AN ELEGANT EXTERIOR

WHEN THE THREE-LITER SUPERCHARGED CAR FORMULA came into force in 1938 (vehicles with 4.5 liter induction engines were also permitted to participate), Mercedes-Benz continued the string of victories it had enjoyed over the period from 1934 to 1937 with a new twelve-cylinder model, the 1938-produced W154, which was used again in 1939 as the W154/M163. The low-slung and elegant three-liter car, which also represented a milestone from the technical point of view, won 11 out of 16 races over two Grand Prix seasons (six victories in 1938 and five in 1939). Rudolf Caracciola took the European Championship in 1938 with the W154, and in 1939 Hermann Lang had the same honor with the W154/M163.

With the introduction of the 750 kg racing formula, designers were forced to obtain the maximum cubic capacity and output they could muster with the available weight limit by constructing extremely light-weight cars. When, in September 1936, the AIACR (Association Internationale des Automobile Clubs Reconnus) laid down the Grand Prix formula to be applied for the years 1938 to 1949, it differentiated for the first time between supercharged and induction machines. Power packs with supercharger were only permitted a capacity of 3,000 cc, while induction engines were able to use a volume one and a half times as great, i.e. up to 4,500 cc. The regulations provided in fact for a sliding cubic capacity and weight scale, although it made sense that the designers would opt to use the maximum permissible overall weight.

The racing department at Mercedes-Benz was just in the process of preparing the 1937 W125 with eight-cylinder in-line engine when the initial design drafts for the future monoposto first came up for discussion in March of the same year. The general management ordered the construction of the Grand Prix car on August 31, 1937, and in March of the following year the W154 with supercharged three-liter V12 engine drove its maiden laps on the Monza track. It was driven on that occasion not only by works pilots Rudolf Caracciola, Hermann Lang, Manfred von Brauchitsch or Richard Seaman, but also by Rudolf Uhlenhaut, the engineer with overall charge of the project. Uhlenhaut was also an excellent driver and achieved some respectable lap times in comparison with those clocked up by the professional pilots. To date, Mercedes-Benz had always built eight-cylinder Grand Prix cars. The V12 concept had previously only been used on record-breaking cars, i.e. the 1935 W 25 R with 5,570 cc engine which produced 736 horsepower and propelled the streamlined car to the grand speed of 372.1 km/h.

In order to gain an idea of the potential offered by an engine whose individual cylinders had a capacity of only 250 cc, the engineers in Unter-türkheim carried out a test using a proven racing model: The 746 cc MG Midget monoposto was purchased from Bobby Kohlrausch in Munich. This small engine (cubic capacity of the individual cylinders = 186 cc) was put through its paces on the test stand and registered an output of

115 bhp at 7,000 rpm, representing a specific power output of 153.3 hp/l. By projecting this value, the three-liter V12 would have to produce some 460 bhp. The new V12 was designed by the group under the leadership of Albert Hess, while Max Werner's team was responsible for the chassis of the W154.

Because of the more compact, and also shorter-lived V12 engine, it was easier for the designers to keep the end face to a minimum, as well as lowering the center of gravity substantially compared to that of the W125. The twelve-cylinder power unit with its 60° fork angle was not mounted using the conventional method along the longitudinal axis of the chassis, but at an angle of 6.5° off the longitudinal axis. This meant a diagonal arrangement of the power transmission, which led to the differential and five-speed gearbox which were mounted as a block at the back left. The drive shaft was also positioned lower at the back than at the front in the W154. The slanting arrangement of the power unit allowed the driver to sit lower down, as he was no longer perched on top of the drive shaft but to the right of it. The outcome was a spectacularly low-slung car which caused a sensation on the racetrack. The line of the bodywork with its wide radiator grille was particularly elegant, and the actual vehicle body (excluding the bump behind the driver's head) was slung lower than the upper edge of the massive Continental tires mounted on the Kronprinz wire spoke wheels. The vehicle was given 400 mm brake drums (in a later version even 470 mm) with magnesium brake shoes. The hydraulic rear shock absorbers could be adjusted by the driver simply by actuating a lever as soon as the tank had been driven relatively empty, reducing the weight on the rear axle.

The V12 power unit under the hood was built from closely packed components, with every inch of space skillfully utilized to the utmost. The bore and stroke dimensions of the almost square-shaped engine were 67 x 70 mm = 2,962 cc. Once again, the traditional Mercedes-Benz engine construction was chosen with the engine block and cylinders made of welded steel elements. The cylinders were welded three to a base plate and encased by a common steel jacket for the cooling water. The V12 comprised four 3-cylinder assemblies, each row of cylinders with its own pair of camshafts. The 30 mm diameter intake and outlet valves, two each per cylinder, were arranged at a 60° angle. The forged crank shaft, which in 1938 was still composed of a single part, was mounted in seven main roller bearings. Each row of cylinders had its own Roots compressor operating at a boost pressure of up to 1.38 at; the two superchargers suctioned the special mixture from a horizontal double carburetor, and the twelve-cylinder was also fitted with a supplementary carburetor. The question of petrol injection was also raised. This was a field in which experience had already been gathered in the construction of aircraft engines, but this solution would require extensive further testing before it could be applied for motor racing. A third of the engine output - between 150 and 160 bhp - was used simply to power the two Roots blowers. When the first test stand trials were carried out on the V12 on February 7, 1938, initially with a compression ratio of 6.0:1, a substantial maximum output of 427 bhp was recorded at 8,000 rpm and at a boost pressure of 1.3 at. During the course of the season, up to 474 bhp were obtained at 8,000 rpm, depending on the compression ratio (6.6:1), boost pressure (up to 1.45 at) and carburetor configuration. However, 8,000 rpm was the absolute maximum permissible speed limit. At higher speeds, unacceptable engine wear or even actual damage were the result. On the racetrack, pilots stuck to a

When the Grand Prix formula came into force in
1938, Mercedes-Benz had a strategic weapon,
the W154 with its three-liter V12 engine, at the ready.
The V12 engine was mounted at a slightly offset
incline, allowing the driver to sit down low next to the
drive shaft. The large fuel tanks were located in
the rear and in front of the cockpit.
The 1939 version of the W154 bore the model
designation W154/M163. The bodywork was flatter
and more elegant. While the 1938 engine had
two separate superchargers, the supercharging effect
was produced in the 1939 model by
a dual-stage blower

maximum of 7,500 to 7,800 revs. Once, a power unit was reported to have risen to an incredible 9,000 rpm as the result of a gear shift error - apparently without further consequences. Another interesting feature of the engine was its incredible battery of no fewer than nine oil pumps. The radiators came from the company Behr, and ethylene glycol with a boiling point of 179° was used as a coolant. The engine guzzled enormous quantities of fuel and oil: For a Grand Prix course of around 500 kph, the oil consumption amounted to as much as 28 liters, necessitating not only refueling but also oil top-ups - something no-body had thought of prohibiting at this stage. The problem of excessive oil consumption was something which the engineers only gradually managed to come to grips with towards the end of the 1938 season, when the forged Mahle pistons were given not only two compression rings but also a second oil stripper ring. Fuel consumption was impressive too: The W154 drained an average of 120 liters per 100 race kilometers of the mixture made up of methyl alcohol for interior engine cooling, acetone, nitrobenzene and ether, but peak consumption rates of as much as 750 liters per 100 km were also recorded. The fuel was accommodated in two tanks, one with a capacity of 250 liters at the back, and a central tank below the pilot's legs between the instrument panel and the engine. This held 150 liters, making a total capacity of 400. During the course of the season, a variety of tank combinations of varying capacity levels were tested. The two tanks were connected at the side by means of large pipes. The idea behind connecting the two was to ensure even draining so as not to upset the weight distribution between the front and rear axle. The pilots were not all in perfect agreement on this point: Caracciola preferred to use a single, large-scale central tank, Lang was in favor of a heavy rear tank which forced the vehicle to

oversteer. In mid-season, a short-rear end car was prepared for Caracciola, whose larger central tank had a capacity of 225 liters and was arranged underneath and to the rear of the cockpit, lending the bodywork a more bulged appearance. The W154s lined up at the start of a race with a filling of between 380 and 410 liters of fuel, making up some 22% of the total starting weight of the vehicle. With the driver on board, the fully fueled car weighed up to 1,325 kg, some 118 kg more than the more bulky W125 of the previous year. At the start of the season, the V12 car weighed 975 kg without fuel, 82 kg more than the 893 kg Auto Union model, which also sported a V12 power unit. The V12 engine itself, of which 19 were built in all, weighed 275 kg (52 kg more than the eight-cylinder M125 which produced up to 600 bhp). Even the tanks added 22 kg to the weight over those used in the W125. The light alloy bodywork was 18 kg heavier, and the chassis with cross members 15 kg - making a total of 70 kg excess weight. The gearbox was fitted for the first time with a fifth speed, which also added several kilos to the overall weight. Despite an output which was 100 to 130 bhp lower and an excess weight of 120 to 140 kg, the W154 still succeeded in more or less matching the lap times achieved with the W125. Due to the five-speed gearbox, better exploitation of torque was possible than in the eight-cylinder model. Using the transmission ratio chosen for the fast Reims track, the V12 achieved a top speed of 99 km/h in first gear at 7,500 rpm, 150 in second, 216 in third, 240 in fourth and 281 in fifth. One problem encountered with the engine was starting unreliability.

The first "Three-liter supercharger formula" season (which despite its name did admit 4.5 liter induction engines) kicked off in the shadow of an impending international crisis. The Monaco, Belgian, Czechoslovakian

Grand Prix venues, the Avus race in Berlin and the German Eifel race, as well as the Vanderbilt Cup race in the USA were all canceled. This left nine races in which Mercedes-Benz was able to compete, six of which saw victories for the Untertürkheim 12-cylinder. Auto Union also had a 12-cylinder in the pipeline, but their rear-engined model did not contend until mid-season, from the German Grand Prix onwards.

The narrow, winding circuit of the town of Pau in the Pyrenees saw the inauguration of the new Grand Prix era on April 10, 1938. However, the venue in Southern France turned out something of a damper on German hopes with the W154 when Rudolf Caracciola was forced by a fuel stop halfway through the race to relinquish his lead to René Dreyfus in a Delahaye 145 with 4,490 cc V12 induction engine. The French 12-cylinder was able to cover the entire race distance without stopping once to refuel. After refueling, Hermann Lang for Mercedes was unable to make good the lead gained by Dreyfus in his blowerless Delahaye with its 235 bhp at 5,000 rpm due to gearbox trouble, and was forced to be satisfied with second place. On May 15, the second race of the season took place in Tripoli. On this occasion, the W154 provided a perfect demonstration of its potential, with Hermann Lang crossing the finishing line before Manfred Brauchitsch and Rudolf Caracciola to make it a hat trick for Mercedes. The French Grand Prix on July 3 was contested by only nine cars on the fast Reims circuit in the heart of French champagne country. This time it was the turn of von Brauchitsch to win ahead of Caracciola and Lang, with a second hat trick for the team. Alfa Romeo's eight and twelve-cylinder racing models did not pose any serious threat to the German manufacturer, although Alfa Romeo had been working for over a year on a 16-valve car which made its appearance at the Italian Grand Prix. At last

the new Auto Union joined the fray for the German Grand Prix on the Nürburgring: Tazio Nuvolari was piloting the new twelve-cylinder for the Auto Union team as a replacement for the popular Bernd Rosemeyer who had died in a speed record accident on the Autobahn on January 28, 1938. On the Nürburgring on July 24th, to the surprise of the Germans, the talented Englishman Richard Seaman unexpectedly notched up his first success in a Grande Epreuve ahead of team-mates Caracciola and Lang, who had been driving relays in the same car. The Swiss Grand Prix held on August 21 ended with a triple victory for Mercedes-Benz in the order Caracciola, Seaman and then von Brauchitsch. The Italian Grand Prix in Monza on September 11 was chosen by Alfa Romeo for the launch of its type 316 with V16 engine, following its previous appearances of the season with its eight and twelve-cylinder models. This new power unit was composed of two eight-cylinder blocks mounted on a common crank case, the system used later in the legendary Alfa Romeo Tipo 158 (also known as the Alfetta). Guiseppe Farina piloted the sixteen-cylinder to second place, while to the delight of the crowd, the small and immensely popular Tazio Nuvolari from Mantua swept to victory in the Auto Union Type D 12-cylinder. Caracciola for Mercedes was forced to be satisfied with third place; the car was also piloted by von Brauchitsch. October 22 saw the end of the Grand Prix season in Donington, England, and another win for Tazio Nuvolari with Auto Union. After various problems for Mercedes-Benz during the course of the race, second and third places were taken by Lang and Seaman respectively.

Work at Untertürkheim towards the 1939 season was restricted to further development and improvements on the W154. The chassis was retained.

135

Of the original 19 built, there were ten type M154 engines left over, and a further four were ordered. The Mercedes-Benz used in 1939 was given the designation M154/M163. The exterior of the new monoposto was particularly striking with its unique flat styling and small oval radiator opening. This was a design concept copied and recopied by other manufacturers over a period of years. One of the most outstanding features distinguishing the 1939 (Type W154/M163) from the 1938 version (W154) was that the new twelve-cylinder was no longer charged by two parallel Roots blowers (one per row of cylinders). For the first time, Mercedes-Benz made use of the two-stage blower, comprising two compressors of varying size operating in sequence. The two-stage blower technique was not new: It had first been employed in aircraft engines during World War One. The double blower in the M163 operated according to the following principle: The first stage compressed the intake air at a pressure of 0.84 at, and conveyed it to the second blower which operated at a pressure of 1.33 at. The main benefit of this arrangement was that the two-stage blower took up only half the output of the two parallel compressors used previously. The boosting effect was not spectacular, but it was possible to reduce the maximum revs to 7,500 or 7,200, which provided optimum operating reliability. Compared to the W154, the W154/M163 was also a fair amount lighter, as the designers managed to reduce the dry weight of the vehicle to somewhere between 898 kg and 918 kg. One super-lightweight model actually weighed in at 855 kg. Of this amount, the engine - now with a compression ratio increased from 6.35:1 to 7.16:1 - alone accounted for 275 kg. In the M163, the crankcase was somewhat wider, and the crankshaft, which in 1938 was stlll forged from a single piece, was now replaced by a split Hirth-type crankshaft. An auxiliary carburetor was used for the power level. The three-liter engine now achieved 480 bhp at 7,200 rpm. This made the cars some 75 kg lighter (no one monoposto was precisely the same weight as the other). On the basis of tests carried out by the radiator supplier Behr, it proved possible to come to grips with the cooling problem despite the much smaller and flatter radiator, which meant an enormous aerodynamic advantage. Work on the chassis included improved brakes, which were now given perforated drums. The fuel tanks were also reconstructed: The central tank contained 185 liters, the rear tank 235 liters, making together 420 liters of special mixture.

The 1939 racing season got under way with partially converted M154 engines. During the first race on April 2nd in Paul the Mercedes entrants took part with the conventional M154 power units. The previous year's defeat was compensated on this occasion by a double victory by Lang and von Brauchitsch. Etancelin in a 4.5 liter Talbot with induction engine came third. For the Tripoli Grand Prix on May 7th, the Italian organizers somewhat unexpectedly changed the qualification conditions in favor of the 1.5 liter voiturette category, which was the traditional sphere of the Maserati 40L and the Alfa Romeo 158. Mercedes rushed to prepare a 1.5 liter monoposto during the winter of 1938/1939. The result was a car smaller than the W154/M163 which was powered by a V8 four camshaft engine with supercharger. To everybody's surprise, Mercedes-Benz even succeeded in winning the event in the hurriedly designed Type 165: Lang won the North African Grand Prix for the third time, just ahead of Caracciola. Two weeks later, on May 21st, the Nürburgring hosted the Eifel Race for Grand Prix cars. Tazio Nuvolari for Auto Union succeeded in making the going tough for the Mercedes-Benz team, but finally Lang took first place ahead of Nuvolari, Caracciola and von Brauchitsch. The Belgian

Grand Prix venue in Spa on June 15th was the scene of a tragic accident and a blow to the Mercedes-Benz team: Richard Seaman was critically injured in a crash caused through wet conditions, and the next day he died in the hospital. Hermann Lang went on to win the race ahead of Hasse for Auto Union and von Brauchitsch for Mercedes. On July 9th at the ACF Grand Prix in Reims, the Mercedes-Benz W154/M163s succumbed one after the other, leaving the field open for a double victory for Auto Union. The next race of the season was the German Grand Prix on the Nürburgring on July 23rd. Paul Pietsch with his Maserati 8CTF initially caused a stir by setting the pace for a brief period. Of the Mercedes team, only Caracciola was still left in the running, and he went on to win the race. The Untertürkheim twelve-cylinder celebrated a hat trick on August 20th during the Swiss Grand Prix on the Bramgarten track near Berne, with Lang taking first place followed by Caracciola and von Brauchitsch.

But by this time the political tensions in Europe had made continuation of the Grand Prix season all but impossible. War seemed set to break out at any moment. One last Grand Prix venue was held on September 3rd on the Belgrade town circuit. The Yugoslavian Grand Prix was contested by all of five cars: two from Mercedes-Benz and two from Auto Union, as well as an almost ten-year-old Bugatti. Nuvolari for Auto Union won ahead of von Brauchitsch for Mercedes. Then came the long-expected announcement of war, which was to place the racing engines and cars and equipment in cold storage for seven to eight years. At the end of 1939, a last stock check was made in Untertürkheim: There were still eight chassis, eight converted type M154 engines and another four Type 163s. The hardware was held in safekeeping in well-concealed hiding places during the war in the Breslau and Dresden areas.

After the war, a few odd Mercedes Grand Prix cars turned up on the other side of the iron curtain. Head of racing at Mercedes, Alfred Neubauer, succeeded in having some of them returned to Untertürkheim, and the American Don Lee managed to extricate a W154/M163 from Czechoslovakia. He took it to America, where it was prepared for the Indy 500 which took place on May 30, 1947. Duke Nalon qualified for the 18th grid position with the Mercedes and was forced to retire after 119 laps with piston trouble, but was classed with a sixteenth position. Don Lee was sent another complete assembly with three cylinders from Untertürkheim, permitting the Mercedes to be prepared for the 500 mile race due to be held on May 30, 1948. This time Chet Miller took the wheel and qualified for slot 19 on the grid, but again the car succumbed to piston failure in lap 108. The essential ingredient that was missing was the familiar hand and practiced eye of the works technicians at the trackside.

The works racing department used three W154/M163s on February 1951 for two formula-free races in Argentina, preceded by test driving on the Nürburgring in preparation during September 1950.

Mercedes-Benz had plans to contest the Indy 500 on May 30, 1951, with the W154/M163. Wind tunnel experiments were actually carried out on a scale model fitted with vertical stabilizing fins (in the actual vehicles, these would have been hydraulically adjustable). However, at the start of April 1951, Head Engineer Fritz Nallinger pulled the pin out of the whole Indianapolis operation, relegating the three-liter V12 Mercedes which had made such a memorable mark on Grand Prix racing in 1938 and 1939, once and for all to the museum.

AMONG VULTURES

Karl Kling, Carrera Panamericana 1952 and the language of the artist

It comes as no surprise to anyone that the artist should originate from Vienna. During his career as an illustrator and painter, Hans Liska worked in Germany and made his home near Bamberg. He was born in 1907 and died in 1983 ("while telling a joke" as the story goes). To judge by his propensity for enthusiasm, he must have led a happy existence, was a lover of landscapes as well as townscapes, an avid theater and opera-goer. His fascination with the subject of movement led him to paint flamenco dancers, bullfights, ballet - making it somehow logical for his volume of sketches to be entitled "Passions".

But first and foremost, Liska was one of the very last of the breed of press illustrators, a "painting reporter of international repute". Under the harsh light of modern media technology the profession was exposed to the ridicule of the high-tech age and retired gracefully and noiselessly from the journalistic scene. It is only in the postmodern age that the painting reporter regains the appreciation which is his due, lending an astounding reassurance and permanence to our con-

ception of history in the making which rings truer than the harsh reality of celluloid.

The beginning of the fifties saw Germany on the threshold of its economic miracle, and one of the movements which so fascinated Liska was the re-emergence of Daimler-Benz and its shining new automobiles. Liska completed a whole series of sketches, drawings and studies of Mercedes as well as other cars, his apprecia-

tion of the arts stretching wide enough to admit the aesthetic beauty of developing technology.

Liska was presumably safely ensconced in or around his studio near Bamberg when on the other side of the Atlantic, 50 miles off Tehuntepec on November 19, 1952, a large bird crashed through the windshield of Karl Kling's 300 SL, injuring co-pilot Hansk Klenk. Initially it was the radio and the news agencies alone who relayed their version of events. In a still abashed post-war Germany, the Carrera Panamericana seemed to gain in size and importance as the news spread, the incident took on sensational proportions as the country warmed to the glory of Mercedes' double victory against the still superior might of Ferrari. The unfortunate vulture had, after all, ventured to attack the winning car, and Kling had still gone on to win, just imagine that.

Just imagine that: a cue for Hans Liska to reach for his pencil if ever there was one. He created what cannot be called the best examples of

Karl Kling, a member of the legendary 1910 generation, captured in 1994 with Hans Liska's interpretation of the Mexican incident in 1952

his work as a press illustrator (his particular skill lay in fine details, which were simply not possible here), but what were to become his most famous, the most frequently reproduced of all his works. The vulture was Mexico, Mexico was the Carrera, and that meant Kling and the SL, the comeback for Mercedes in the motor racing world, a new regard for Germany after the war beyond the confines of Europe...

What really happened? Mercedes contested the race with Kling, Lang and Fitch mainly against Ferraris driven by Ascari, Phil Hill, Bracco and Villoresi. On paper, a contest it could hardly hope to win, and one which

Number 4 was the right number to back: Karl Kling, Hans Klenk, Mercedes 300 SL. Kling crossed the final finishing line with a lead of no fewer than 37 minutes over Hermann Lang, followed by a sea of Ferraris and Lancias. Left: The nearest Mercedes tire depot was seventy kilometers from the scene of the incident. Here, the glass splinters were carefully removed and Klenk received provisional treatment

from the edge of the road in perfect compliance with the rules of normal everyday through traffic, but had evidently not reckoned with the speed of Kling's approach.

The pain suffered and the endurance demonstrated by his courageous co-pilot was treated with altogether greater reverence, his description of the atmosphere as the winning car crossed the finishing line is moderation itself: "The enthusiasm of the crowd was altogether great". Kling did experience something of a problem with the winner's trophy, though, an enormous bronze monument which did not somehow seem to fit in with the engineer's mode of life. So he pre-

placed the Mercedes team under enormous pressure. In the heat of the first leg, the Mercedes pilots saw not only their tires giving way left and right, but also suffered the ignominy of witnessing a large bird hurtling through the windscreen of the Kling car, injuring co-pilot Klenk in the face. He lost consciousness under the blow, and came round only to insist that Kling keep going, KEEP GOING. He held out the 70 kilometers to the next tire depot, and also gritted his teeth through the following 200 kilometers to the next finishing line, his blood-caked face steeled against the wind which rushed through the now glassless windshield frame. A new windshield was mounted overnight, this time sporting additional protective bars. During the course of the race, Kling went from strength to strength. The Ferraris were dogged by a variety of problems, and Kling's increasingly offensive driving tactics ended with a final spurt to victory across the finishing line in record time. His average speed over the 3,113 kilometers was 165.1 km/h.

The world was impressed, his home country in raptures. And then came this picture!

Whatever it was that sparked off Hans Liska's imagination, it cannot have been Karl Kling himself. He behaved with collected calm throughout his much-publicized drama, then as 20 or 40 years after the event. He confirms the official statistics as to the bird as he had done to the press all those years ago (the dead animal was jammed behind the seats all the way to the tire depot, with its "wings tickling" the pilots in the back of the neck): 115 cm wingspan, 50 kilos in weight.

That a creature weighing as much as ten fatted geese could hardly be a master of aerobatics is a detail which has paled into insignificance over the decades. Liska's vulture is, in any case, one of the more wiry variety. It may not even have been a vulture at all, Kling prefers to refer to it as a "large bird", but one which at any rate had no experience with motor racing. It had lifted off

sented it either to a museum or to someone, he no longer remembers which.

But Kling's expression really lights up for the first time when he recalls how it was with the spare windshield. It is the sort of story which clearly appeals to him, and which he tells like this:

"Neubauer was fairly worked up when we reached the finishing line for that leg of the race in Oaxaca, and tried in vain to put a call through. Finally, he stormed off to the post office to wire the Mercedes agency in Mexico City (where a central depot of SL spares had been set up). The Mercedes agent in the capital had already long since heard about the incident on the radio, and reacted straight away by hiring a private plane to send a windscreen to Oaxaca. Neubauer came puffing back from the post office to the hotel, where the news had just come in that there was a windscreen waiting to be picked up at the airport. Neubauer, with a self-satisfied grin, beamed: 'That was quick'."

MAY 2nd, 1955

THE YEAR WHICH SAW THE MOST GLORIOUS OF GRAND PRIX TRIUMPHS ALSO GAVE THE SLR ITS MOST MEMORABLE DAY.
STIRLING MOSS AND DENIS JENKINSON HAD AN IDEA

"THE MECHANIC CAME BEARING A BOWL which contained hot water, and was also carrying a cake of soap and a towel. It was meant for me, especially for the lad Stirling to wash off the layer of grime and dust which had been sprayed onto my face. It was my first test drive for Mercedes in Hockenheim in the late autumn of 1954, and it was a sight so impressive I will never forget it: A mechanic with a bowl of hot water."

Stirling Moss was 24 years old when he was summoned. No other expression quite captures the way in which Alfred Neubauer delivered his "urgent message" to London.

The next incident which sticks out in Moss's memory is a cry from the depths of a DC 6B winging its way to Argentina (this could only be the description of a technical enthusiast, who even 40 years later cannot bring himself to say airplane when the machine was a DC 6B): "We heard a droning noise coming from behind which could only mean one thing: The portly Neubauer was stuck in the toilet and was helpless to extricate himself until Hans Herrmann and I ran to free him - but it turned out to be nothing more than a joke. Neubauer regarded his figure with a healthy sense of humor."

Moss loved his work for this team which offered scope for fun but at the same time provided all the undoubted benefits of legendary German efficiency, and a far greater feeling of being looked after than he had experienced with the English or Italian teams he had worked in. Of cour-

se he was faced with more paperwork, time schedules, itineraries and the like, but Stirling Moss recalls that "it was simply great to get your 20 dollars daily allowance in the right currency every time, as well as the precise amount to pay for the ferry or tollgate, plus an extra dollar every day to have the car you drove to the race track washed. Honestly, an extra dollar every day - so that a Mercedes works driver should only ever be seen in a clean and shiny car. I put the dollar in my pocket and washed the car myself - which gave me double the enjoyment."

Seen in the light of motor racing history, all Grand Prix victories and the string of successes clocked up by Stirling Moss are outshone by the single most outstanding event of his racing career: The Mille Miglia in 1955, which he contested in the Mercedes 300 SLR.

There are two fundamental reasons why.

Two years before its abrupt and unforseeable end, the Mille Miglia had reached the zenith of its immense popularity. While reckless bravado and pure speed were called for on the one hand, the race also demanded an immense fund of experience and know-how if the ins and outs of the 1600 kilometer course were to be braved without risk to life and limb. The sensation that was caused when a young puppy of an Englishman managed to achieve this with greater success than the Italian heroes of the day (Maglioli! Castellotti!! Taruffi!!!), or Fangio at the high point of his career, was something never to be forgotten - impressing the Italians, capturing

*Stirling Moss,
Mercedes 300 SLR
Le-Mans version.
In the wake of the
Grand Prix
triumphs which
marked the year
1955, the roadsters
too were in a class
of their own,
winning the
Sportscar
Championship
although not
seriously on the
agenda that year*

the imagination of the world and sending the British into unbounded ecstasy.

And the other reason? Bit by bit, the world came to learn about the courageous new idea which helped the Brit to his unprecedented victory. Two men had entered into a partnership in which each placed his life in the hands of the other. In the event this was no exaggeration, and the fact that we were able to meet both men alive and kicking just under 40 years later is the living proof that the experiment was successful.

Meet Mr. Jenkinson: Denis Jenkinson, who is never Denis but always simply Jenks to all who know him. Jenks has now reached the ripe age of 74, lives in an idyllic village in Hampshire (like something off the top of a biscuit tin), and has been writing for over a year for *Autosport* after a 40-year journalistic career with *Motor Sport*. Evidently not one of the fly-by-night generation.

Jenks is small in stature, which was no doubt a boon during the five years he spent in the European motorcycle scene as a sidecar passenger. Eric Oliver and he won the 1949 World Championship with Norton, and it was around this time that he first took up his pen as a motor racing journalist, later to become the most famous of them all, a veritable monument to his profession as the man who won the Mille Miglia with Stirling Moss.

Jenks met Moss in 1954 in Pescara when he was just borrowing a Maserati to drive around the long track. Could he come along for the ride? – Mmph. Moss was somewhat more handy with the throttle than he might otherwise have been. It is a pleasure to drive with you was all the response he was able to provoke from the collected Jenks. As Moss had already witnessed his driving companion in action on the tarmac as someone who evidently found some kind of unnatural enjoyment in twisting and turning on what is little more than a surfboard on wheels, this convinced him: This guy is mad.

But it was just such a one that he was looking out for a few months later when he had his Mercedes contract in his pocket and an eye on his chances in the Mille Miglia.

Right from the beginning of their association, Moss and Jenks were of the same opinion: For two green young Englishmen there was little prospect of winning such an unequal contest unless they were able to devise a way to make up for the local knowledge and experience of the Italians. The idea of pace notes, meaning a series of danger warnings, had already been devised and put to good use during the Carrera Panamericana. The Lincoln team was also reported to have employed the services of a drawing of the course wound round a drum. What Moss and Jenks had in mind was something along these lines but taken much further, a system which would permit them to foresee every nook and cranny of the course.

Training took place over a period of several weeks, interrupted periodically by Stirling's racing weekends at some location or other around Europe. It is almost a nightmare scenario: Every Mille Miglia practice round meant 1600 km exposed to the rigors of the Italian traffic, straining to achieve the highest possible speed, flat out, mile for mile at up to 250 km/h, sometimes in normal cars and sometimes enjoying the comparative luxury of the SL or SLR.

Jenks took notes, Moss had them typed up in his office and collected together in a neat folder - a pointless exercise as it turned out, as the concentrated information only came to life when accompanied by Jenks's inimitable sketches and signs and symbols, his own special code which

no-one else could read or decipher. So he transferred his notes himself, spending countless hours on all fours before a continuous roll of paper.

Mercedes mounted an on-board intercom system in the training car and Jenks began to read out the results of his labors. This worked fine until Moss began to gain speed and appeared to turn deaf in the process. At a moment of acute danger, he simply failed to hear what was being said to him.

A doctor who had been involved in examining pilots undergoing space training experienced a similar phenomenon: In life-and-death situations, the human brain seems to possess the ability to call on untapped reserves of potential in the life-saving activity or function at the expense of the remaining senses. You can run faster than the normal boundaries of your strength will allow without feeling anything, or when your life depends on your eyes, your powers of vision are intensified to the extent that you are no longer able to hear. One could argue that modern rally driving practice gives the lie to this theory - here, acoustic perception goes on working even when the other senses are stretched to their utmost. In this case, though, the pilots are working to a system which has been developed and refined over decades and which has become second nature to them. But even here, there have been extreme accidents over the years which continue to defy explanation - the most obvious example being the death of Finnish Henri Toivonen and his co-pilot in 1986 in Corsica.

So the team threw the on-board radio communication system out the window and instead concentrated on translating the records into hand signals. Initial training took place on the Hockenheimring, and was continued on private trips in a normal limousine. From around 15 hand signals, Jenks construed a special language which Moss was able to regi-

ster and respond to in any position. Moss had extremely good eyesight which allowed him to pick up an incredible degree of detail over a wide angle. Jenks would make his signals just at the right point of his visual field without having to twist himself into contortions.

The final draft of Jenks's transcript encompassed a continuous paper roll five and a half meters in length which could be accommodated in a specially designed aluminum box and wound on using a roller mechanism. The viewing window was made of perspex and sealed with Sellotape to keep out the rain.

But this was only one equation of the duo's winning formula. The other aspect of consideration was the role played by reason and emotion, the lengths to which mutual trust should be taken in a life-and-death situation. This was not just another race or some rally or other. This was the single most dangerous road race of all times, one that took no consideration of towns and villages and crowds of unprotected spectators lining the route, and which urged its participants 'round blind corners and over uncharted hill-brows which could send an SLR flying at 280 km/h with 7500 revs into the unknown - provided the man with his foot on the gas was guided by an unswerving belief that when Jenks said FULL SPEED AHEAD, then full speed ahead it should be.

Moss: "Of course he had nerves of steel which was helpful. And he was fearless to the point of self-surrender."

"To the point of self-surrender, Jenks?"

"With a man like Moss at the wheel, yes. With just any old driver, no. I am certainly not a fatalist. I experienced air raids at the aircraft research center where I was stationed in the war over a period of years. That is what I call dangerous. What followed was peace time. Just think, peace throughout Europe - that put an end to danger as I understood it."

"Wasn't it possible back in 1955 to foresee that the Mille Miglia was simply too dangerous, and that a disaster of the kind that actually happened two years later was just a matter of time?"

Denis Jenkinson: "A race was a race. The danger which was uppermost in our minds was that we might lose. I came from the craziest field of motor racing. After five years on Europe's racetracks in a motorcycle sidecar you give up wasting too much thought on the dangers of motor racing. I experienced some tracks like Barcelona - Montjuich, for example, which were lined by human crash barriers - in other words it was the spectators which formed the edges of the track. And when I leant out of the sidecar to take a narrow corner, my head would be practically moving along next to the shoes of the spectators. As long as no-one had changed places, I passed by the same pairs of shoes every time I went past. It never once occurred to me that this could be dangerous - it was simply normal. And when I had more time to consider matters - say for five seconds or so on the straight - I was simply happy at being able to crouch down and listen to the engine singing aah, my baby sings beautifully. And I was proud, too, because I was a mechanic as well as being a co-pilot, and I was responsible for creating those beautiful tones. I simply felt intense pleasure at being part of it all."

"In other words, you never felt fear even as the co-pilot who was sending Stirling Moss over a blind hill-brow at 280 km/h?"

"Firstly, the race proper was actually a relief in as far as we were finally free of the need to contend with the normal everyday traffic. We were able for the first time to experience the unsullied pleasure of letting it rip without fear of encountering a donkey cart around the next bend. Secondly, it is probably impossible for anyone now to imagine what it meant: A 25 year-old and highly motivated Stirling Moss at the helm of the most incredible of racing cars. Moss was incredible too, possessing what seemed to be superhuman powers - it was the perfection of an art form. For me to be there to experience it at first hand meant first and foremost fascination and a tremendous enthusiasm. Time has shown that Moss was not invulnerable. But for me he was - at least during those ten hours, seven minutes and forty-eight seconds on May 2nd, 1955. So everything depended on my not making an error. And I was absolutely determined not to let the side down.

"Of course we had both considered the fact that we were each committing ourselves to the skill and judgment of the other. We got over this hurdle by fooling around. Stirling would say: 'Hey, do you realize that if you make a mistake, I am a dead man? Just you remember how famous and important I am, if you please!'

And I would answer: 'But in my life there is no-one more important than me. Don't worry, I will be taking pretty good care of myself.' "

Denis Jenkinson continues:

"What was new about the system we developed was the way it extended our possibilities for communication. Most previous systems had stopped at simply notifying danger. This was naturally still the most important aspect, for example to provide adequate warning about bumpy road surfaces which could end in a damaged car, or tight corners coming

immediately after the blind crest of a hill. We had three different graduations for tricky curves and the relevant hand signals to match: *saucy, dodgy* and *very dangerous*. We then went a stage further to belay any last doubts about the possibility of going all-out in any particular situation. In this way we would be able to gain, say, three seconds here, and other three seconds there.

"Stirling had previously declared his intention of placing his absolute trust in me. Later, he admitted that he had still entertained a last shred of doubt, but this had flown to the winds pretty soon after the start. There was one point which he remembered slightly differently to the way I indicated it to him. When he saw that I was right, he gave up any attempt to join in the thinking part of the partnership and put all remaining doubts out of his mind altogether, abandoning himself fully to my instructions. This situation of utter mutual trust allowed him to reach the absolute peak of his driving ability.

Our feeling of sheer happiness at the start of the race was typical of our attitude. It ran like some sort of a scientific experiment, almost like a space mission: Two men have prepared together in total mutual trust for a task in which they enjoyed all the backing of the world - or rather in our case the not inconsiderable support forthcoming from the Mercedes machinery with its meticulous planning and preparation. But the moment arrives when all the support in the world can no longer help you, when you are both alone with your fate. You are shot out into space."

The article published by Denis Jenkinson in the English magazine *Motor Sport* is counted one of the classics of motor racing literature. Quite apart from the monumental value of its subject matter, what distinguished the article from the sensationalism of modern press reporting is its natural approach, the clarity and simplicity of its structure, and the very humbleness of the author.

Before you read the last quarter of that memorable article, just one or two of the more vital statistics about the race: There were 521 entrants, the first of whom started on their intrepid journey from Brescia on the evening of May 1st. The Moss/Jenkinson team started on the morning of May 2nd at 7.22 as part of the highest powered vehicle category. There were three other Mercedes entries: Fangio as the absolute favorite, as well as Kling and Herrmann. Simply because of the impossibility of each car keeping track of where it stood in the race (at certain checkpoints pilots were able to ascertain their current standing, but as a rule they drove "blind" and were forced to wait to hear the grand total at the end), there was no kind of pecking order whatsoever. For the German works team, the most important of its opponents were Taruffi in the 4.4-liter Ferrari, Castellotti and Marzotto in 3.7-liter Ferraris, Perdisa in a 3-litre Maserati and Peter Collins for Aston Martin. The Mercedes 300 SLR was equipped with 290 horses and tuned for a top speed of 272 km/h at 7500 rpm in fifth gear. The course was 1,606 kilometers long, Brescia - Pescara - Rome - Florence - Bologna - Brescia.

We are now on the return journey and will climb into the cockpit with Moss and Jenks in Siena, with the kind permission of the author. The headline is indicative of the matter-of-fact approach adopted by Denis Jenkinson: WITH MOSS IN THE MILLE MIGLIA. The almost complete dearth of paragraph breaks is in keeping with the original and reflects Jenks's style of continuous narration of events.

Denis Jenkinson, Motor Sport, *1955*

"At the Siena control we had no idea of whether we were still leading or not, but Moss was quite certain that Taruffi would have had to have worked extremely hard to catch him, for he had put all he knew into that last part of the course, he told me afterwards. Never relaxing for an instant he continued to drive the most superb race of his career, twirling the steering wheel this way and that, controlling slides with a delicateness of throttle that was fairy-like, or alternatively provoking slides with the full power of the engine, in order to make the car change direction bodily, the now dirty, oily and battered collection of machinery that had left Brescia gleaming like new still answering superbly to his every demand, the engine always being taken to 7,500 r.p.m. in the gears, and on one occasion to 8,200 r.p.m., the excitement at that particular instant not allowing time for a gear change or an easing of the throttle, for the way Moss steered the car round the sharp corners with the back wheels was sheer joy to experience.

On the winding road from Siena to Florence physical strain began to tell on me, for with no steering wheel to give me a feel of what the car was going to do, my body was being continually subjected to terrific centrifugal forces as the car changed direction. The heat, fumes and noise were becoming almost unbearable, but I gave myself renewed energy by looking at Stirling Moss who was sitting beside me, completely relaxed, working away at the steering as if we had only just left Brescia, instead of having been driving for nearly 700 miles under a blazing sun. Had I not known the route I would have happily got out there and then, having enjoyed every mile, but ahead lay some interesting roads over which we had practised hard, and the anticipation of watching Moss really try over these stretches, with the roads closed to other traffic, made me forget all about the physical discomforts. I was reminded a little of the conditions when we approached one corner and some women got up and fled with looks of terror on their faces, for the battered Mercédès-Benz, dirty and oil-stained and making as much noise as a Grand Prix car, with two sweaty, dirty, oil-stained figures behind the windscreen, must have looked terrifying to peaceful peasants, as it entered the corner in a full four-wheel slide. The approaches of Florence were almost back-breaking as we bounced and leapt over the badly maintained roads, and across the tramlines, and my heart went out to the driver of an orange Porsche who was hugging the crown of the steeply cambered road. He must have been shaken as we shot past with the left-hand wheels right down in the gutter. At speeds up to 120-130 m.p.h. we went through the streets of Florence, over the great river bridge, broadside across a square, across more tramlines and into the control point. Now Moss had really got the bit between his teeth, nothing was going to stop him winning this race, I felt.

´This is going to be fantastic,´ I thought, as we screamed up the hills out of Florence, ´he is really going to do some nine-tenths plus motoring´ and I took a firm grip of the ´struggling bar´ between giving him direction signals, keeping the left side of my body as far out of Moss's way as possible, for he was going to need all the room possible for his whirling arms and for stirring the gear-lever about. Up into the mountains we screamed, occasionally passing other cars, such as 1900 Alfa Romeos, 1100 Fiats and some small sports cars. Little did we know that we had the race in our pocket, for Taruffi had retired by this time with a broken oil pump and Fangio was stopped in Florence repairing an injection pipe, but though we had overtaken him on the road, we had not seen him, as the car had been hidden by mechanics and officials. All the time I had found it very difficult to take my eyes off the road. I could have easily looked around me, for there was time, but somehow the whole while that Moss was really dicing I felt a hypnotic sensation forcing me to live every inch of the way with him. It was probably this factor that prevented me ever being frightened, for nothing arrived unexpectedly, I was keeping up with him mentally all the way, which I had to do if I wasn't to miss any of our route marking, though physically I had fallen way behind him and I marvelled that anyone could drive so furiously for such a long time, for it was now well into the Sunday afternoon. At the top of the Futa Pass there were enormous crowds all waving excitedly and on numerous occasions Moss nearly lost the car completely as we hit patches of melted tar, coated with oil and rubber from all the other competitors in front of us, and for nearly a mile he had to ease off and drive at a bare eight-tenths, the road was so tricky.

Now we simply had to get to Brescia first, I thought, we mustn't let Taruffi beat us, still having no idea that he had retired. On we went, up and over the Raticosa Pass, plunging down the other side, in one long series of slides that to me felt completely uncontrolled but to Moss were obviously intentional. However, there was one particular one which was not intentional and by sheer good fortune the stone parapet on the outside of the corner stepped back just in time, and caused us to make rude faces to each other. On a wall someone had painted "Viva Perdisa, viva Maserati" and as we went past in a long controlled slide, we spontaneously both gave it the victory sign, and had a quiet chuckle between ourselves, in the cramped and confined space of our travelling hothouse and bath of filth and perspiration. The hard part was now over, but Moss did not relax, for it had now occurred to him that it was possible to get back to Brescia in

A view from the camera of the legendary motor racing photographer Louis Klemantaski, who co-piloted with Paul Frère for Aston Martin in the 1955 Mille Miglia

Denis Jenkinson with the box containing the wisdom which made all the difference on May 2, 1955

157

the round 10 hours, which would make the race average 100 m.p.h. Up the long fast straights through Modena, Reggio Emilia and Parma we went, not wasting a second anywhere, cruising at a continuous 170 m.p.h. cutting off only where I indicated corners, or bumpy hill-brows. Looking up I suddenly realised that we were overtaking an aeroplane, and then I knew I was living in the realms of fantasy, and when we caught and passed a second one my brain began to boggle at the sustained speed. They were flying at about 300 feet filming our progress and it must have looked most impressive, especially as we dropped back by going round the Fidenza by-bass, only to catch up again on the main road. This really was pure speed, the car was going perfectly and reaching 7,600 r.p.m. in fifth gear in places, which was as honest a 170 m.p.h. plus, as I'd care to argue about. Going into Piacenza where the road doubles back towards Mantova we passed a 2cv Citroën bowling along merrily, having left Brescia the night before, and then we saw a 2-litre Maserati ahead which shook us perceptibly, for we thought we had passed them all long ago. It was number 621, Francesco Giardini, and appreciating just how fast he must have driven to reach this point before us, we gave him a salutary wave as we roared past, leaving Piacenza behind us. More important was the fact that we were leaving the sun behind us, for nice though it was to have dry roads to race on, the blazing sun had made visibility for both of us very tiring. Through Cremona we went without relaying and now we were on the last leg of the course, there being a special prize and the Nuvolari Cup for the fastest speed from Cremona to Brescia. Although the road lay straight for most of the way, there were more than six villages to traverse as well as the final route card stamp to get in the town of Mantova. In one village, less than 50 miles from the finish, we had an enormous slide on some melted tar and for a moment I thought we would hit a concrete wall, but with that absurdly calm manner of his, Moss tweaked the wheel this way and that, and caught the car just in time, and with his foot hard down we went on our way as if nothing had happened. The final miles into Brescia were sheer joy, the engine was singing round on full power, and after we had passed our final direction indication I put my roller-map away and thought "If it blows to pieces now, we can carry it the rest of the way." The last corner into the finishing area was taken in a long slide with the power and noise full on and we crossed the finishing line at well over 100 m.p.h., still not knowing that we had made motor-racing history, but happy and contented at having completed the whole race and done our best."

So much for Denis Jenkinson. Then there was the thing about Fangio's pills.

Their Argentine teammate had given Moss and Jenkinson some pills which were intended to improve stamina and endurance. Later, Fangio revealed that these had been made of all natural substances - maybe a hand-down from the Indian tradition - but that the most important thing was belief that the pills would help overcome fatigue. However that may be, Moss (and Fangio) had taken the pills, but not Jenkinson. On the evening after the race, amid the jubilant celebrations taking place in the Mercedes camp and a party thrown by Count Maggi, Jenks betook himself to bed. Moss, nothing daunted, got into his own car at two in the morning and drove alone through the night. He was in Stuttgart in time for breakfast.

Moss/Jenkinson, Mercedes 300 SLR, passing through Ancona on their way to achieving the fastest Mille Miglia of all times

FATHER'S CAR IN BERLIN

Edzard Reuter remembers the Mercedes 170 S:
Official car of the Mayor of Berlin

This is the day on which not diplomats and generals will be doing the talking. Today is the day on which the people of Berlin will raise their voice in an appeal to the whole world... Peoples of the World, in America, England, France, Italy! Look at this city and acknowledge that you must and can not sacrifice this city and its people! ...We have done our duty, and will continue to do our duty... Peoples of the world! We appeal to you to do your duty too!"

The words of Ernst Reuter on September 9, 1948, in what was to become a famous address to a gathering of 300,000 people in front of the ruined Reichstag building. It was the time of the Berlin blockade and the allied airlift, whose dimensions are best called to mind today by the record number of 927 aircraft landings in a single day.
After two periods of incarceration in concentration camps, emigration to Turkey from 1935 to 1946, and a recall to serve as Municipal Minister of Transport to Berlin, Ernst Reuter finally became Officiating Burgermeister of the city and a legendary figure who helped shape the face of history in divided post-war Berlin. His son Edzard was born in 1928.

The 1950 Mercedes 170 S Convertible, today admired as a symbol of the impending economic miracle in the Mercedes-Benz Museum, was Ernst Reuter's official car. Edzard Reuter remembers:
"Father was enthusiastic about cars, but it was only in later life that he actually possessed one of his own. It was a Volkswagen, some-

where around 1951. I remember how proud he was of it. My parents used it for the only holiday they ever went on, to Italy. After my father's death in 1953, it became my first own car.
Despite his enthusiasm, he was a terrible driver. He had trouble shifting down an unsynchronized transmission. The car used to jerk all over the place and my mother would complain.

At around the same time as the Beetle, my father had the use of a 170S convertible as an official car, of course complete with driver. This is what he used for all important journeys. Longer trips to ´West Germany´ through the Russian occupied zone were always done in that car for reasons of principle as well as convenience. There was repeated talk of the possibility that the roads to the West might be blocked off again after the end of the blockade, and so a particular effort was made to continually highlight the claim to free passage through the zone. Added to all that, my father simply adored being driven, particularly in what was by all intents and purposes a luxury convertible whose

handling performance couldn't be praised enough in those days. Whenever the opportunity arose, he had the roof opened. He made an appealing picture sitting there in the Basque cap which he had taken to wearing during the years in Turkey.

The love he cherished for cars, even if (or perhaps because) he did not find it an easy matter to get to grips with them, was something I must have inherited from him. I have vague but comforting early memories of car journeys as a child with a favorite uncle. And another thing I remember from very early on is a burning curiosity and an interest in everything that bore the name Mercedes. I remember quite clearly one single occasion in Turkey as a child, it must have been around the beginning of the forties, being taken for ride in a breathtakingly beautiful Mercedes. Never since have I experienced the inside of a car so consciously as I did then - the beauty of the leather upholstery and the splendid instrument panel. It was dark, and the inside lights were switched on. The atmosphere was one of indescribable elegance and sophistication. I firmly believe that it was this occasion which crystallized my passion for cars in general and for Mercedes in particular. This passion never left me, which is why this convertible from the post-war era brings back so many positive emotions."

"From a very tender age, I developed a curiosity and passion for everything bearing the name Mercedes." (Edzard Reuter)

FOUR-STAR COLLECTION

RALPH LAUREN AND HIS AESTHETIC QUARTET:
THREE SLS AND AN SSK WHICH HAVE EARNED THE RIGHT TO A FEW SPECIAL TOUCHES

RALPH LAUREN needs no introduction. Within only a few years he has established a name for himself which, like those of Dior, Lagerfeld, Armani or Kenzo, quickly became synonymous with success and the art of good living on an international scale. His weakness for the automobile is one of the less publicized facets of Ralf Lauren, who has put together a personal collection of exquisite quality and variety which includes, for example, four models from Mercedes-Benz.

And if this collection is known only to a favored few, it is hardly surprising. The time Ralph Lauren is able to dedicate to his automotive charges is short indeed, his invitations to visit them few and far between. His collection comprises around forty automobiles and is housed at a location somewhere between the outermost tip of Long Island and Westchester County in the State of New York.

There are two important conditions which go some way to explaining Ralph Lauren's unique skill: One is his pronounced preference for America - he was born in New York and has always lived and worked there - and the other is a highly developed sense of intuition when it comes to making the right decision. Choosing a car is something he will never delegate to anyone else. Needless to say, Ralph Lauren is on familiar terms with the experts on all the different marques, all the particular models - and he has never hesitated to take advice. But the final decision is his and his alone. A circumstance which is all the more remarkable consider-

ing the number of different offers he must receive. The care and maintenance of this illustrious fleet is in the capable hands of mechanic Ron Barnes, whose considerable experience was gathered in the British motor racing scene. And a fleet it is indeed, not a museum: Every single vehicle in the collection is registered and ready for the road, the layout of the garages is such that shunting is hardly ever necessary to get to the car you want to drive.

Barnes and his wife Zoe, whose quarters are only a stone's throw away, take care of such unlikely stable-mates as a Bentley 4.5 supercharger and two Ferrari Testa Rossas dating back to 1958 and 1961, a 1957 Porsche RSX, and a Jaguar D-Type bought by Ralph Lauren on the death of its owner, Duncan Hamilton, an Alfa Romeo 8C 2900 Convertible Touring Car and "the" Bugatti Atlantic, a single-seater Maserati 250 F "Piccolo" and an assortment of various Ferrari 250 GTs, including the 1960 limousine, a Spider California from 1961, a '62 GTO... the list is endless.

Ralph Lauren is fond of asking: "Which car do you think is still missing from the collection?" Not an easy one to answer - especially bearing in mind that one of the objectives must be to retain the widest possible variety. But our host has a few ideas of his own which are about to be revealed...

Mercedes is represented in the collection by four different models: An SSK, which we will come back to later, and three 300 SLs. No fewer

The legendary silver-gray paintwork is softened by yellow highlights.
The supple natural leather used by Ralph Lauren for the interior appointments is generally used in the clothing industry. Removal of the bumper flanges has created a less obtrusive silhouette, and a more elegant look for the wheels is provided in the form of rudge hubs

than three cars of a model of which more than 3,000 were produced - isn't that going over the top for a collection of this scale, whose other models are either unique or at most "limited editions"? It seems not.

Firstly, because the value of a collector's item has less to do with its rarity than with its special features and its quality. As far as this goes, the 300 SL has an awful lot to offer, and especially the models owned by Ralph Lauren. The 300 SL is a vehicle with its own special fascination, not only because the doors hinging onto the roof open up to give it the appearance of a massive beetle about to take flight - a feature which incidentally gave the bodywork its nickname "Butterfly". Quite apart from its striking appearance, everything else about the 300 SL is a law unto itself. Its design, the technology behind it, its whole history - all are indicative of the achievement of excellence. The fact that the name Mercedes-Benz has come to be synonymous with qualities such as efficiency, success and progress is due in part to the 300 SL, whose development was dogged by enormous problems right from the beginning.

The end of World War II. There was nothing left but reminders of past achievement at the Stuttgart company whose production base in Untertürkheim lay in ruins, its production in total disarray, in a Germany that was torn apart and bled all but dry. Given the many other pressing priorities demanding attention, the production of luxury limousines was forced to take a back seat. When asked to consider priorities, it went without saying that what were needed were commercial vehicles and series-produced cars - certainly not custom-built, prestige models to pander to an elite minority. The first great breakthrough achieved by the Daimler-Benz Board of Management was in mustering the foresight to see beyond this dismal horizon. The company took the momentous decision to adhere to

The 300 SL Coupé with its aluminium body was restored precisely according to the "original"; Only the pattern of the seat covers is of Ralph Lauren's own designing

its existing policy, to continue to cultivate an image founded on out-standing technological achievement and luxury, given an additional polish on occasion by the production of spectacular racing cars. Without abandoning the production of commercial vehicles and the small family saloon Type 170, the marque with the three-pointed star brought out the luxury limousine 300 as early as 1948 - a brazen move indeed for those times - and decided to stage a comeback in the motor racing scene. The man in charge of racing, Alfred Neubauer, and engineer Rudolf Uhlenhaut checked out every possibility open to them. At the highest end of the sport, Formula One, the regulations only permitted two engine types up to 1953: A 4.5 liter induction engine and a 1.5 liter supercharged engine. Time was too short to allow Mercedes to develop and optimize a specific vehicle. ven by the veterans on the Nürburgring, he simply but firmly refused to have any more to do with this particular venture.

But the racing department did succeed in gaining approval from on high, and in particular from the Head of the Automobile Department, Fritz Nallinger, for a return to Formula One for the 1954 season. In the meantime, a less ambitious schedule was planned to help return the wheels of routine back smoothly into motion. This was based on a success-

ful mixture comprising equipment at a reasonable price and the greatest possible "Mediatizing", or put in more modern terms, creating an optimum cost-to-performance ratio. As Manufacturers' Championships were not yet held at this stage - they were introduced for the first time in 1953 - Neubauer restructured the program to a series of 5 venues which he chose on the basis of the prospective audience and their geographical position in countries which represented important sales markets for the company's commercial strategy. In chronological order, these were the inimitable Mille Miglia in Italy, the Berlin Grand Prix, a race organized in the run-up to the Swiss Grand Prix, the 24-hour Le Mans race in France, the Jubilee Race on the Nürburgring, prior to the German Grand Prix - that was all the country had to offer by way of racing venues in those early days - and finally the Carrera Panamericana in Mexico, the race which took place over the border from the US but which within only two years was well on the way to gaining the greatest following among Americans...

The Mercedes developed in record time to take part in these various venues was given the internal designation W194 and was presented to the press on March 12, 1952. It had already been named the 300 SL, although it had but little in common with the illustrious "butterfly" that was

Only the aluminium coupé is fitted with the traditional white steering wheel. The other two 300 SL models sport a wooden steering wheel which Ralph Lauren had specially designed with four delicate struts, reminiscent of a Mercedes racing car and a Bugatti rolled into one

to follow it. The six-cylinder in-line engine with its three-liter displacement - hence the designation 300 - was derived from a limousine launched onto the market by Mercedes a year previously. Taking its origins back a step further, it could be traced to the V12 power unit of a pre-war Messerschmitt. The most striking special feature of the engine was that the intake and exhaust were both located on the left-hand side. The lateral camshaft which, in the limousine, used pistons to actuate the suspended valves, was located directly above them. However, despite its three double carburetors supplied by Solex or Weber, the engine achieved a horsepower of only 170 at approaching 6,000 revs. Compared to its contemporaries, the 3.4 liter six-cylinder engine of the Jaguar C-Type, for example, or the V12 4.1 liter engine of the Ferrari America, the result was somewhat on the modest side. The team of engineers from Stuttgart led by Uhlenhaut solved the problem by stripping away the car's "excess ballast" – which brings us to the reason for the "L" for "lightweight".

After a respectable second place in the Mille Miglia, the Mercedes 300 SL (W 194) went on to achieve its big breakthrough. Max Hoffmann, the American marque importer with the keenest business sense, was convinced that the USA offered a market for a 300 SL series version, and he was able to gain the backing of the Stuttgart management for his idea. The other positive outcome to emerge from the successful racing campaign was a decision to launch a Formula One monoposto (W 196 R) for the 1954 season and also to develop a sports car (W 196 S) to follow one year later. Although the series model of the 300 S was given a higher internal type number (W 198), it had nothing in common with its eight cylinder-engined predecessors. The W198 was more like a direct successor to the W 194 although miraculously enough without being really similar to it.

The last prototype of the road version 300 SL caused a major stir when it was presented in February 1954 at the New York Motor Show. A change to the injection system had bumped the output up in one fell swoop from 170 to 215 bhp, and the car had taken on a far more refined and civilized air all round. A case example of how much the Gran-Tourismo class automobile owes to motor racing. Another challenge which the 300 SL (W 198) took comfortably in its stride was the new design. No other manufacturer could have succeeded in integrating the radical but artistic modifications to the original silhouette with the same degree of harmony and skill. The changes at the front were particularly striking, those at the rear and on the roof less so. In its own way, the 300 SK represents an intriguing affront to all that is orthodox in automobile styling. Its emphatic wheel openings, for example, the squashed engine hood or the solid bumpers. The new car carried the day - and no-one was ever to dare to lay hands on the bodywork of the 300 SL again. Ralph Lauren proudly presents the two most important models in his collection: a standard coupé (1,400 cars produced) and a roadster (1,850 produced), both fitted with the particularly effective-looking rudge hubs. He had the two models restored by the specialist Paul Russell, although as some subtle integrated details indicate, not entirely without consulting his own tastes: The gray metallic paintwork enlivened by yellow highlights, a wooden steering wheel with four fine struts reminiscent of a Bugatti and the same time of the Mercedes racing cars; gold-colored natural leather instead of the less supple leather customarily used, and the bumpers, which relieved of their top-heavy flanges. The aluminum coupé, the twenty-second to be made of a total series of twenty-nine, was restored by Ralph Lauren to its original state – almost by way of an apology for his own originality.

Ralph Lauren designed the costumes
for the film "The Great Gatsby".
He could have given Robert Redford the loan
of his Mercedes SSK at the same time

While the success of the 300 SL can be measured in figures which reflect a brilliant marketing achievement, piece numbers play no role at all for the S-Class produced during the twenties.

On the basis of the short 1923 "K" model, the engineer Ferdinand Porsche designed a flat sports version in 1927 which was given the internal reference number W-05 and the designation S (around 164 models were built). This design was later further developed to become the SS (154 built), and the even shorter SSK (42 built), and finally the lighter-weight SSKL (12 built). The only statistics of any real significance when we consider the S-Class of that era are those which describe its performance. These offer plenty of conclusive information about the engines used, all of which shared the following characteristics: Six in-line cylinders with overhead camshaft, double ignition, two internally produced updraft carburetors and a supercharger actuated by the accelerator. The career of this M-06 engine got under way with the values 15/70/100 - in plain language 15 taxation bhp, 70 bhp without supercharger and 100 bhp with the supercharger in operation. It reached its zenith with the values 27/240/300 in the SSKL in 1932, alongside only a modest increase in cubic capacity from 6.8 to 7 liters.

The specifications of Ralf Lauren's SSK at 27/180/250 speak for themselves. What

mean a lot more are the emotional ties between the man and the vehicle. Before Ralph Lauren's time, this SSK worked its special magic on other collectors - men of the caliber of Tom Perkins from California and English Sir Anthony Bamford to mention only the last two of the car's owners.

Both these two had been so unconditionally taken with the car that they had not even attempted to find out who had designed the unique bodywork. According to company records, it appears that the SSK no. 36038 was finished in the summer of 1930 and dispatched to Tokyo where it waited in vain for a buyer. From there, the SSK was transported to Rome, finding its way finally into the fleet of Count Trossi in Biella in Piemont. Carlo Felice Trossi was young and wealthy, and had a weakness for cars and motor racing. He had come to the attention of Enzo Ferrari, who had appointed him President of the Scuderia Ferrari which not only represented Alfa Romeo at the trackside but was also responsible for its commercialization in the Emilia-Romagna regions. Can the Count have committed the unforgivable sin of unfaithfulness to his marque? Alfa Romeo naturally had a series of fascinating 2.3-liter eight-cylinder engines to offer - but nothing that could come within miles of the SSK's proud seven liters! Trossi managed to obtain a dispensation from on high for his beautiful Mercedes. And still nobody knew who had given it this breathtakingly elegant bodywork.

Who can it have been, this obvious-

ly talented genius who transformed the bulky roadster, implanting nothing but four fenders and a streamlined rear end? The answer to this mystery finally came from Buenos Aires following a report by photographer Michael Zumbrunn published in 1984 in the magazine "Automobiles Classiques". Ricardo Polledo, former Director of the Argentine Automobile Club and one-time owner of the

car, was in no doubt about the identity of the mystery coach builder. It can have been none other than Jacques Saoutchik, the Ukrainian sheet metal artist from Paris whose work included a large selection of models from Stuttgart. Polledo clearly remembered the car and the adventure he experienced with it in 1949. Having always regretted selling his SS some years previously, he could not resist the temptation to put in a bid for the SSK following the death of Count Trossi. Although negotiations with the Count's heirs were brought to a speedy conclusion, Ricardo Polledo was unable to obtain an import permit - something which was absolutely imperative in Peron's Argentina. In the end he had no choice but offer the car up for resale. Because the chances of finding a potential buyer in Europe at that time were just about zero, he decided to pack up his acquisition - together with a crate of spares and parts which took up as much room as the car itself - and send it off to New York restorer Charles Stich, one of the most successful dealers of the day. Only a short time later, the black SSK had become one of the most sought-after collector's items of all time.

In 1992, Ralph Lauren decided to give his prize possession a face-lift following its restoration ten years previously by Anthony Bamford. Needless to say, the job was taken on by Paul Russell. Nine months later, a newly born SSK emerged from the womb of its workshop near Boston just in time to pick up the "Best of Show" award in Pebble Beach. The restoration could not have been more discreet: The spoke wheels and the red interior appointments had given way to black. A striking detail was the reappearance of the 1932 Roman license plate in its familiar place at the back left. Russell had adhered like glue to the instructions provided in the workshop manual, which under the heading "Regular checks" offered advice such as "Completely dismantle the vehicle at intervals of 18,000 km....".

Can we still be justified in talking about a "limited edition"? And if you care to return Ralph Lauren's question about which car is still missing from his collection, he will not have to think for long. "A Mercedes W 154", is his unhesitating reply. Which all goes to prove that a collection is never complete.

PROFESSOR SAFETY

Béla Barényi, in Automotive Engineering's Hall of Fame

Stuttgart in 1932. A cold day in December. A young man in a suit that is rather the worse for wear gingerly approaches number 24, Kronenstraße. The address is none other than the design office of Prof. Porsche, the celebrated German automobile designer. Our hesitant young man enters, a battered suitcase he carries in one hand stuffed with plans and ideas. He politely requests permission to present them. The secretary summons a few gentlemen, among whose number is Erwin Komenda, who had worked together at the drawing board with the young engineer at Austro-Fiat. So they are already acquainted. The eager twenty-five year-old begins to explain his ideas with the aid of the sheaves of papers he has brought along. Alongside bodywork drawings, the papers also reveal a concept for the design of a new type of people's car. The gathering of elders are listening to him patiently, discussing the ins and outs of the designs when the door opens and in walks Porsche himself. He honors the young designer and his papers with not a single glance, simply asks a few brief questions of his employees and then makes his retreat. History could well have taken another course had Barényi possessed the presence of mind to address Porsche directly. As things stand, despite the general interest in his suggestions, Bela Barényi is made to understand that there is no opening in these difficult times for another man in the design office, so he reluctantly returns the majority of the papers to his suitcase. A few he leaves behind, including the papers describing the

people's car, or Volkswagen concept, for closer inspection. He had actually only stopped off at Stuttgart on the off-chance on his way from Vienna to Paris, as without a secure position he felt that not even the most slender chance should be missed. But this is only one more of the many disappointments he has had to contend with, and so he makes his way to the railway station hoping that his next opportunity will bring the breakthrough he is waiting for. One of many unsuccessful applications – and yet this episode is to affect his life in a way he could never have imagined possible.

Change of scene. In 1992, peak viewing time, a number of the private channels broadcast an advert which looks more like the beginning of an intriguing documentary. "No-one in the world

has given more thought to automobile safety than this man", the commentator informs us, as the camera follows the progress of an elderly, white-haired gentleman in a camel coat as he walks through the Castle Gardens at Schwetzingen. Anyone just in the process of channel-hopping to avoid the usual nerve-racking bombardment of adverts is stopped in mid twiddle, captured by the person of Bela Barényi and by the message which is coming across. Over a period of decades, Barényi and his research work have conceived and optimized design features relating to automobile safety on behalf of Daimler-Benz AG. Inventions which in the final reckoning came to benefit not only Mercedes drivers but as a consequence all other drivers everywhere. Barényi was a pioneering spirit whose ideas were often

40 years and more ahead of their time. Barényi's realization that the completely rigid car passes on its full kinetic energy to its passengers in case of impact, and that consequently zones should be created which will absorb this energy came like a revelation to the world of automotive engineering.

Why should a young man back in 1920 dream about achieving perfect automobile safety when the rest of his generation was cheering on the streamlined convertibles and roadsters of their racing heroes? Barényi, who was born in 1907 as a citizen of the Austro-Hungarian Monarchy, spent a carefree childhood in the castle-like property of his grandfather

Bela Barénji at 87: A bastion of support for Churchill's maxim of "No sports"

Fridolin Keller, a wealthy tradesman and supplier to the court and the armed forces. It was here that he made his first encounter with the automobile. His grandfather owned an Austro-Daimler, naturally chauffeur-driven. He was allowed to sit up next to the chauffeur during the family's regular Sunday jaunts out, and his observant eyes took in every detail of the driver's movements at the wheel.

As a boy, Béla spent a happy childhood surrounded by his mother, grandmother and eccentric aunts who used to induce the pet monkey to perform tricks during afternoon tea by bribing it with pieces of chocolate cake. In 1914, this idyllic existence came to an abrupt and unpleasant end. Barényi fell victim to an inflammation of the hip joint, which left him with a stiffness in his right leg.

World War I not only put an end to the Austrian Monarchy, but at the same time the business empire of his Grandfather. His own father was killed in the war, leaving the family of five accommodated after the summer of 1920 in a modest apartment in Schwenkgasse 7/9, District XII in Vienna. The family reached such desperate financial straits that Barényi was forced to abandon his school education for lack of funds – for of course in those days going to school cost money, and this was a commodity in short supply in the Barényi household. He went as a practical trainee to the company Fischl, Trenkler, Weiser & Co., an automobile and machine factory. This new environment aroused his technical interest, which was not only affirmative but already highly critical too. One of the things that struck Barényi when he saw his first Ford T-Model was that the hub of the steering wheel was formed to a point, and was practically aiming towards the driver's chest. The result of his deliberations was the construction of a bob sleigh with a safety steering wheel. This marked the be-

ginning of a path which the young designer was to consistently tread right through to the end of his working life: the promotion of passive safety in the automobile.

But there was another design idea committed to paper by the then twenty-five year-old Béla Barényi which was to exercise a lasting impact: The Volkswagen, or people's car. As early as 1926, he put forward design drawings as part of the final presentation at the end of his training period. The plan he submitted at that time already featured many of the main design characteristics of the later VW: the rear-mounted flat engine with horizontal cylinders, the central tubular frame, longitudinally arranged crankshaft and layout of the transmission in front of the axle with the engine behind. Barényi was concerned, too, with engine design. His final presentation submitted in 1926 also contained plans for a six-cylinder petrol engine designed to provide an output of 50 hp at 3600 rpm.

Fresh out of technical college, he was fairly bursting with ideas. He designed, he drew, he published his ideas in automobile journals. He designed cars, cigarette lighters, salt spreaders. But despite all his efforts, the search for work in those difficult days was hard and unrewarding. In 1927 he found himself without employment, after which he was engaged briefly by the Steyr plant and then by Austro-Fiat in Vienna. In his search for an opening he traveled in 1931/32 to Vienna, Paris, Stuttgart and Frankfurt. In Paris, he made the acquaintance of René Charles Faroux, who actually published an article about his ideas in the French car magazine 'La Vie Automobile'. Despite general interest, no-body was able to offer him employment. It was only after talking to Josef Ganz, publisher of the Motor-Kritik magazine, who enlisted the help of an acquaintance, the designer Röhr, that Barényi was finally able to settle down into employment with Ad-

ler in Frankfurt. Through his work with Adler, the young engineer came into contact with the GETEFO, the German Society for Technical Progress, which took him into its employ in 1934. He was now based in Berlin, where he worked on a number of projects on behalf of the GETEFO. Motorcycle frames for Norton, elastic suspension systems for the trains of the Brussels State Railway, and various vehicle projects, including one for the company Tatra-Nesseldorf/CSR, where he worked in cooperation with Hans Ledwinka. His work involved Barényi in chassis design, in problems relating to vibration and noise insulation, cell vehicles and rubber-to-metal welded joints, which represented a vast improvement over the silent block as a bearing method for chassis components and engines.

At long last, the day of the long-awaited interview at Daimler-Benz arrived. The Director and later Board Member Dr. Wilhelm Haspel summoned him for an interview in Stuttgart. The interview, which lasted far longer than envisaged, ended by Haspel engaging Barényi with what has become a frequently quoted justification: " A company like Daimler-Benz cannot live from hand to mouth. Mr. Barényi, your ideas are 15 to 20 years ahead of their time. In Sindelfingen, you will be placed under a glass bell jar. What you invent will go straight to our patent department." His employment under these conditions gave Barényi what amounted to a university status within the company. It was a highly unusual situation which gave him the freedom to work practically undisturbed.

During this period and as the war progressed, alongside the Experimental Car II he worked on the "Concadoro" and "Terracruiser" projects, which incorporated all the essential elements which contributed towards the safety cell concept with crush zone, which was patented in 1952.

The first car to feature this technical revolution was the rear fin Mercedes, internally designated the W 111. At a very early stage, Barényi realized that there can be no single solution to the problem of safety in automobile construction. What good are seat belts and airbags if the rigidity of the bodywork offers insufficient protection and if the front and rear structure fail to absorb sufficient kinetic energy through selective deformation? So when the Professor (the title was conferred upon him in 1989 by the Austrian President) watches today's car advertisements extolling the virtues of individual safety features he is often unable to suppress the smile which plays about the corner of his mouth; side protection, safety roof (the pagoda roof in the 230/250/280 SL/W 113), safety doors, safety steering wheel, safety steering column and roll-over bar - these were things he was thinking about

before the idea of passive safety had even been raised by other automobile manufacturers. Even when he had been working for his diploma, he had occupied himself with the subject of steering. He was quick to realize the dangers inherent in the lance-like steering column as the single most dangerous component for the driver in case of an accident. He presented the perfect solution to the steering wheel dilemma in 1960 with a split steering column whose ends were joined by an easy-give deforming body as a coupling element.

In 1952, he became the target of accusations trumped up in the worst possible journalistic taste. Richard von Frankenberg and Horst Mönnich accused him in their books, a biography of Ferdinand Porsche and a book about the home town of Volkswag-

en, Wolfsburg, of unjustly claiming to be the inventor of the Volkswagen, an honor they believed to accrue to Porsche. Barényi's only interest in the matter was his honor as inventor. To have accepted such an accusation unchallenged would have made his prominent position at Daimler-Benz all but untenable. It was this consideration which prompted him to enter into a court case which was to last three years, leaving him financially and mentally drained.

The case finished happily for him with a confirmation before the patent division of the Local Court of Mannheim that he was the inventor of the basic Volkswagen concept. His right to make this claim has been immortalized for all to see on a plaque in the Deutsches Museum in Munich.

Today, an idea Barényi was working on at the end of the fifties and beginning of the sixties is moving back into the limelight at Mercedes-Benz: A small car offering a safety standard and spacial conditions comparable to a luxury limousine. The K-55. There was even a prototype built, although the concept never made it to the production line, not being sufficiently in line with prevailing tastes among Mercedes customers at the time. Barényi was never at the head of a massive department, preferring instead to lean on his motto of quality rather than quantity: What he wanted was a small number of sound, outstanding colleagues. Little wonder, then, that top designers like Paul Braque and Bruno Sacco were members of his team. His life's work has met with acclaim from many quarters, but the greatest accolade of all came in 1994, when he was honored with a place in Detroit's Hall of Fame alongside such names as Gottlieb Daimler, Karl Benz, Rudolf Diesel, Ferdinand Porsche and Robert Bosch as that which he had always worked towards being: The father figure of passive automobile safety.

A monument to Integral safety thinking based on the interaction of countless detail solutions: Barényi's "Pagoda roof"

THE LONG MARCH

The 1000-mile spectacle – the Mille Miglia 1994: One of the last and very special adventures cherished by a man in love with beautiful cars and the sensation of speed.

Uwe Brodbeck relives the Mille Miglia

I t was just like old times. Somewhere on the narrow, winding road from Siena to Castellina in Chianti country, sleek silver racing cars flew past like an emotionally charged whirlwind, the faces behind the steering wheels lit up in childish delight. And delighted they were.

They stood on the brakes, they screeched around corners, they tussled and struggled as if their honor depended on it, they slap-ped their co-pilots on the thigh for joy as they had done when all this had been in deadly earnest. Four kilometers later at one of the checkpoints, the infernal trio – a Mercedes 300 SL gullwing, an SL prototype, and a Porsche 550 Spyder – pulled up after having just flown neck and neck past what was actually an impassable but belatedly noticed steward. Stirling Moss peeled himself out of his doorless prototye and engaged Porsche pilot Hans Herr-

man in a bear-hug, gasping: "Wasn't that fantastic!" And it was. These are the moments which turn a Mille Miglia into an experience of the unforgettable kind, engraving an indelible impression in the memory. And it is habit-forming. So they all tell us, those lucky ones painstakingly selected and invited by the Automobile Club di Brescia, which guards the integrity of this very special event like the German Bundesbank watches over the interest rate, accepting just 330 cars from a total of 800 applicants. Those few have the chance to share in an experience, to be part of an exclusive club sharing a common goal: To drive aged, beautiful and fast racing and sports cars from Brescia to Rome and back in pursuit of a childhood dream.

Of all the ceremonial magnificence surrounding the Mille Miglia, the splendid stages set up in Ferrara, Rome, Siena or Florence, it is Brescia which sums up the very essence of what this very special race is all about. Once a year in this medium-sized town not far from Milan, Mille Miglia fever breaks out in earnest, bringing its annual invasion of automobile delights in every shape and form and everything that goes with it: Overfilled hotels, crowded restaurants, congestion, traffic jams and the screaming of highly-tuned engines echoing unfiltered through the narrow lanes of Brescia's old quarter.

O n the Piazza Vittoria right in the heart of Brescia, surrounded by buildings of outstanding architectural beauty, we attempt to thread our Mercedes-Benz 300 SL gullwing, as every year, through an unbelievable mayhem comprising yellow taxis, vegetable transporters, service vehicles and racing cars towards the check-in. In the familiar search for our starting number, papers and the obligatory sponsor bag in bright Mille Miglia red, we discover Hans Herrman on the left pushing his works car, a deli-

Before the start in Brescia; Uwe Brodbeck and Gerd Schüler, Mercedes 300 SL

spectacular and loudest family get-togethers imaginable - 330 resplendent racing veterans from the 1927 OM 665 Superba proudly bearing number one to the 1957 Ferrari 250 TR racing under number 330, which incidentally was flown in all the way from Hong Kong for the occasion.

The age-old ritual begins. The teams with the lowest starting numbers get ready for take off, the usual good-byes are said and the advance party disappears into the darkness, filling the night air with a pre-war cacophony of backfiring and low-pitched growls. Memories flood back: The excitement of the Mille Miglia novice, nerves at breaking pitch, the naiveté which had us waiting at the starting line hours before our time, wasting fuel by nervous tread-ing on the gas pedal. With all the self-assured ease of practiced Mille Miglia veterans, I and my co-pilot Gerd Schüler, a one-time successful Alfa Romeo and Ford works driver, pick our way not a moment too soon to the 30,000-strong teeming mass of

Parc fermé in a tumbledown castle on the edge of Brescia. 330 teams were nominated to take part in the Mille Miglia

En route for the starting ramp:
Mercedes SSK piloted by Grashei

cate Porsche 550 A Spyder from 1956, towards the check-in point. The 1.6 liter power unit with its venomous 150 bhp simply refuses the indignity of crawling along at walking pace - this is not what it was designed for, after all.

Issued with the starting numbers 295 for the Porsche, 284 for my SL, and 286 for the silver-blue Porsche 356 A Carrera belonging to Swabian Paul-Ernst Sträble with its notorious license plate WN - V2, a real Stuttgart trio has come together: Soon to become a quartet with the addition of Stirling Moss, almost a neighbor with the number 303. In between, an assortment of Ferrari 500 TRs, a 250 GT and an unashamedly good-looking Maserati 450 S slot into their appointed places. The 400 bhp monster takes over 300

km/h easily in its stride, and awakens deep-down emotions in British Stirling Moss: In 1957, he succumbed to a broken brake pedal 14 kilometers from Brescia in just that very car, putting paid to his hopes for a repeat of his legendary victory of 1955 with the Mercedes 300 SLR.

There is a unique sense of camaraderie about the Mille Miglia. Most treat it as a yearly pilgrimage, a recurring and almost sacred obligation from which nothing could ever deter them. They come from around the globe, the Ferraris, the Lancias, Bugattis and Mercedes packaged in cotton wool and embedded lovingly in the bellies of Jumbo Jets. The check-in and the evening buffet in a tumble-down castle are among the most colorful, most

officials, pilots, spectators and hangers-on swarming around the brightly lit starting line. A bag left at the hotel turns our nonchalant appearance into a hectic rush after all, which ends in us stranding our silver gull-wing in a cul-de-sac.

No matter, here in Brescia – at least at Mille Miglia time – the

High point just before Rome: Passo de Terminillo (2213 meters)

normal rules of traffic count for nothing, for participants at any rate. A friendly policeman straddles his Moto Guzzi and escorts us complete with flashing lights through an astonished Brescia, the wrong way up one-way streets and past other equally unimportant impediments to the periphery of the starting ramp, where we gratefully thread our way through the long snake of automobile hardware precisely between number 283, a Lotus, and 285, a Ferrari 500 TR all the way from Japan.

*A*n estimated 30,000 people throng to the edge of this never-ending ramp every year for the start, which is traditionally *held on a Thursday. The crowd takes you into their hearts, even if you are not piloting one of the shiny red Ferraris or a Lancia or Fiat. The wave of enthusiasm is overwhelming, and engulfs one and all, from number 1 right through to 330. The line-up is under starter's orders as we roll our gullwing onto the floodlit ramp. Amid a flood of applause and the deafening staccato of an Italian announcer we set off into the night.*

It is way past 10.00 p.m., and we have had a long day. For a change conditions are dry, and the SL's headlamps light our way comfortably through the darkness. I recall one occasion years before in streaming rain when one windscreen wiper broke off shortly after the start - luckily on the passenger's side. Midnight is

The wintry impression is borne out by the thermometer reading: Minus 1.5 degrees at the top of the Monte Terminillo pass

182

Brescia to Rome and back: The Mille Miglia means a two-day 3D cinema extravaganza for teams and spectators alike

marked by the roar of a passing Maserati whose exhaust pipes would have drowned out the trumpets of Jericho hands down. We are suddenly wide awake again, our leisurely fourth gear and 100 km/h making way to a lively third as we warm to one of those challenging stretches which are so characteristic of the Mille Miglia.

It is long past midnight when we spot the lights of Ferrara, marking the first 179.70 km of our journey. Pilot and co-pilot can sink back into their seats: After all, Thursday had been a working day like any other back in Stuttgart. Despite the lateness of the hour - and this sums up the inexplicable fascination of what they call the "Reliability Race" Mille Miglia – the brightly lit backdrop of Ferrara's old quarter is lined by an unbelievable welcoming crowd at two in the morning. The fatigue of the last few hours is dispelled in an instant, the pilots are infected by the excitement and no-one thinks of going to their hotel. Italian wine and local specialties flow liberally on all sides, pilots and co-pilots toast each other from plastic beakers filled with red wine and look forward to the following morning.

The night is short. Far too short. But nobody seems to be the worse for wear. A crowd of around 20,000 has gathered to wish us well on the next leg of our journey to Rome. The start is punctual to the second, and our SL purrs its way with its accustomed precision along the road towards Rimini and Pesaro, the speedo swinging casually over the 200 km/h mark every now and again.

The urge to down a cool drink and a salami sandwich or two turns our lunch break into an unexpected highlight: On the seemingly endless stretch after Pesaro, Gerd Schüler discovers a promising road-side restaurant and urges an unscheduled pitstop. It was to be a memorable meeting: Who should stop just moments later but Messrs. Sträble, Moss, Herrmann, to be shortly joined by guest driver Jochen Mass who noticed the cars and managed to brake his 300 SL just in time to join the party.

Some time later and after being treated to some of the best from the rich store of yarns kept by these old hands of the racetrack, we

Driving through downtown Florence is one of the Mille Miglia's most precious moments

set out towards Ancona way behind schedule. There would be a lot to tell - but perhaps it is best to preserve a mantle of silence over all those red traffic lights, no overtaking zones and one-way streets which may or may not have been overlooked that afternoon. Perhaps a good word should be said about the role of the police, not only here but throughout the whole of the historical Mille Miglia: No stopping in front of red traffic lights is tolerated, slow-coaches in 50 km/h speed limit zones are forced up to at least 100, and in built up areas, oncoming traffic is forced practically off the road to make room for us.

The Mille Miglia 1994 is drawing to a close. We reached Rome by midnight, starting again the next morning on the way back to Brescia, experiencing Siena and particularly Florence as the two climaxes of the journey. And I will never forget how we romped through the sun-drenched streets of Florence with Paul-Ernst Sträble's silver-blue Carrera and Hans Hermann's delicate Spyder in tow, or how the Porsche's Sebrings left their own very special thunderstom between the houses lining the route.

After 16 hours on the road and late on the Saturday night, we see the name Brescia signposted for the first time. It is pitch dark, and Hans Herrmann's works Porsche has a generator failure. He drives sandwiched between two colleagues, using their lights to guide him at a cool 180 km/h towards Brescia, something unthinkable back in those days. Then, it was each man for himself, now it is a contest between friends. Naturally enough, as Sträble points out, the historical Mille Miglia has turned into something of a "watchmaker's rallye": Seconds and fractions of seconds, special tests along the route and no longer simply a question of the car with the fastest time. But despite all that: Between those special tests and the rubber hoses to be driven over with split second accuracy, the Mille Miglia of old lives on. Old hands like Moss, Sträble or Mass all agree: "It is no longer the winning that is important, it is the taking part".

LAST TIME IN AUTOPOLIS

ABOUT PICASSO AS A POOR MAN AND SCHUMACHER AS AN ASTOUNDING NOVICE.
PLUS: A TRIBUTE TO THE GREAT, THE INIMITABLE SPORTSCAR

1989 to 1991:
The silver Sauber Mercedes.

A RIDE WITH THE WORLD CHAMPION. Jean-Louis Schlesser is sportscar champion of 1989, and the Sauber Mercedes C9 with the bodywork number 05 was the car whose debut in Le Mans in 1989 was the prelude to four victories in the capable hands of Schlesser/Mass: Jarama, Nürburgring, Donington and Mexico. A World Champion's car.

We are in Paul Ricard in the South of France, the lap times for the C9 plus passenger would be around 1 minute 14 seconds, I am told - some two seconds slower than Alain Prost's last Formula One pole position time. That is about as close as you will get to that Formula One feeling sitting in the passenger seat.

The C9 is revved up and raring to go. I am kitted out from top to toe in all the racing driver gear, the left gullwing door is open, beckoning.

To get me into the cockpit would take some shoehorn. The driver is allotted a touch more space, and Wendlinger – who is 1 meter 87 like myself – only just fitted in with clothing to spare. And anyway he weighs 75 kilos to my, um,…

The colossal proportions of the car's exterior (1980 mm wide) should not be confused with the cockpit, which I can only describe as a capsule in the center. You have to swing your right leg over a side sill more like a doorstep at over half a meter wide, and thread it down the narrow shaft while your left foot is still standing firmly on French soil. Then a tortuous twist of the right knee to forces it down under the edge to allow the rest to follow. We discover that shoes are definitely out of the question. OK, no shoes. Then belting up, mmph. An attempt to close the roof down over my helmet leaves me understanding more about sardines. I am able to discern the accustomed twinkle in Schlesser's eyes through the visor of his helmet, a reassuring sign. What a job for him!

The confinement is a nightmare. My head is forced over to one side, thrust into the helmet which is wedged absolutely tight. I handed in my legs to the vise up front and have not really felt them again since. For the first few seconds I seem to have forgotten all about breathing, and now I have to make up by gasping ineffectually for air. Whose crazy idea was this? Perhaps I should just shut my eyes until it is all over. Just keep breathing, I tell myself, breathe in and out, that is the most important thing. I am not at all frightened about what could happen - accident-wise, I mean - only that I might pass out or suffer a stroke through constriction, perhaps. They actually measured my pulse just as I was getting in (those Mercedes boys really think of everything) and nobody died yet from a pulse of 72. As long as I make sure I get my ration of oxygen; I must keep breathing.

Jean-Louis turns his helmet to look in my direction. "Ready for take off?" he intimates with a raised forefinger. My answer goes something like:

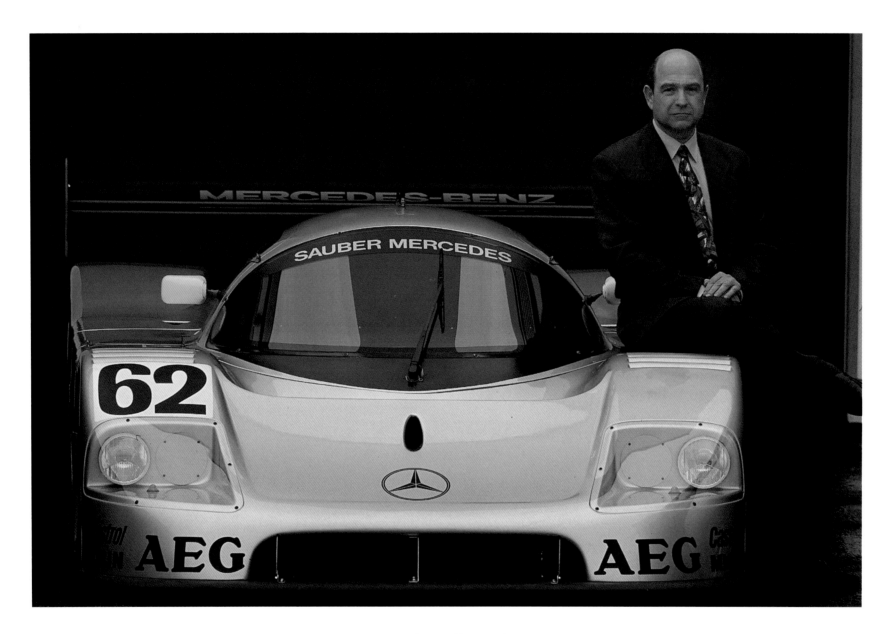

Peter Sauber and his machine:
Sauber-Mercedes C9,
World Championship Sports Car 1989

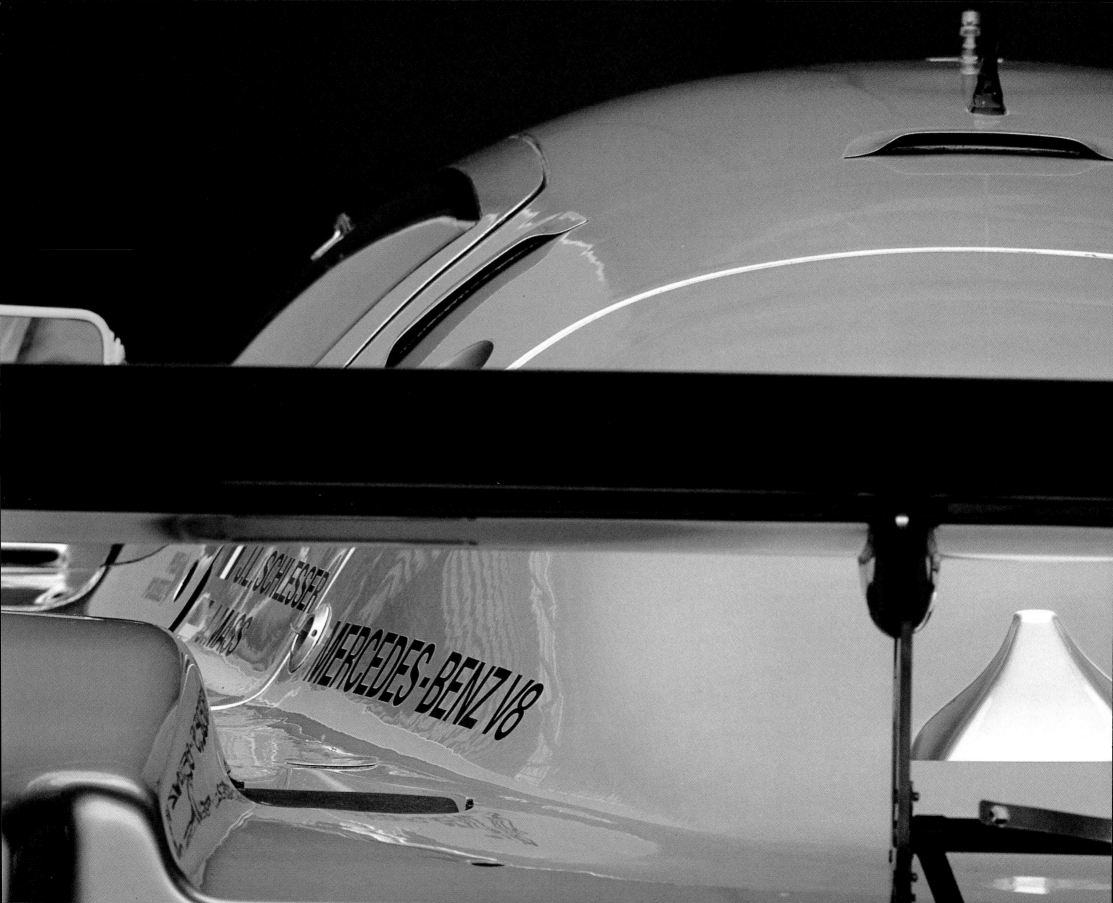

"Cch-hhh-hh-hh."

Jean-Louis presses the starter, the mechanics detach the umbilical cord linking us to mother pit, the car lowers onto its hydraulic jacks, roars and is off.

I am aware that we will be accelerating from zero to 100 km/h in just under three seconds, the knowledge makes my breath even shorter. The shake-up seems to have loosened my helmet, my head is now almost straight. But still: The confinement! I have never been closer to another man than I am to Jean-Louis - we seem to be one package with gear shifts going on somewhere in the middle. With a giggle verging on the hysterical, I notice that we are not driving straight on (along what used to be the Mistral straight), but are turning off to the right in a way designed to rob me of yet more breath. I am paralyzed, un-able to do anything but think about the necessary respiration. I concentrate on breathing in slowly and regularly, and once we emerge from an enormous tangle of leftandrightandgoodnessknowswhere my breathing is clearer, the view is clearer, we brake into the right-hand corner before coming to the long straight. Then up go the gears, into sixth, and I know: Somewhere in the region of 300 km/h over the starting and finishing line, now breathing easier.

Braking into the right-hand corner at the end of the start and finishing line. I have heard tell that this is supposed to be a whole new situa-

tion for racing drivers: That tough step on the carbon brakes. It brings a whole new quality to their perception, a completely different kind of sensation .

Now I can tell you what it is really like.

It has nothing, not in the remotest, to do with the feeling of braking, of slowing down. There is not the slightest transition between braking and not braking. It is like driving into a brick wall and coming out the other side with a new lease of life, you can still steer, you go on driving, left, right. The rest is pure bliss. Perhaps there is nothing in the world to compare being driven by a man who really knows what he is about in a car conceived and built for one purpose and one purpose only: to stretch the very limits of physics. The impacts and the bumps are heavenly, and when the centrifugal force grabs you, you could shout for joy. At first I intended to study Schlesser's movements in detail, as well as the needle fluctuations on the rev counter, but I soon gave it up, gave in to the pure sensation of it, hoping again and again that Jean-Louis would never stop, another lap, and another.

When we finally rolled home into the pit, when they opened the roof and started the major task of extricating me (someone whipped off my glove and pressed my hand onto the pulsometer: 131, cool as a cucumber almost) I was happy through and through. What a profession, was the first thought I was able to collect rationally, how lucky I am.

By Easter 1989, Peter Sauber had progressed to the extent that Werner Niefer called for the silver paint pots to be placed at the ready. It was the greatest possible blessing to be hoped for from this marriage of the Swiss C9 with the Swabian V8: It seemed that a state of the art had been reached where it was legitimate to start talking again about the Silver Arrow.

There followed two years of plenty, and they were followed by a lean year.

The last race in Autopolis, 1991.

Autopolis, the very sound of it! That sound alone tells half the tale of an incomparable race. And the thing about Picasso: A once-in-a-lifetime experience.

We distinguish between the blue-is-blue theory and what we can perhaps call the candlelight hypothesis. The first is supported by the mighty backing of the maestro himself ("You are the best there is in the world... a color to outshine all other colors the bluest of all conceivable blues."). Which adds up.

The second hypothesis sounds more like the fantasizing of some self-important art experts, but in actual fact it is really so: When Picasso was too short on funds to feed his oil lamp (pre-1910), he used to hold a candle in his left hand and paint with his right. Biographer Roland Penrose mentions the "weak illumination offered by the candlelight and its tendency to dampen the effect of yellow" as a possible reason for the bluish tones which characterized Picasso's work over a period of several years.

Jeepers, I thought as I cast my eye over the picture, perhaps they were right about the candlelight after all. The whole picture appears to still be flickering, and it is a mass of blue. The bride is blue, the Harlequin is blue, so are all the shades except the foreground. That is brightened by candlelight, but we do not see the candle - Picasso was only holding it, and did not put it in the painting. Perhaps when we look at it nowadays, we should only do so with a candle in our left hand.

Outside, I heard a Mazda screeching, followed by the sound of a Jaguar braking. I ought to look how Wendlinger is getting on, I thought, and walked outside.

Only briefly beforehand, we had been disgruntled to read it in the papers (disgruntled from the standpoint: "There will soon be nothing left in the West that does not belong to the Japanese."): Tomonori Tsurumaki had put around 55 million dollars on the table for "Pierrette's Wedding", a masterpiece from Picasso's blue period. Tsurumaki also owns a Renoir, van Gogh, Monet, Bonnard and Magritte, being a lover of pictures.

A lover of cars he is too, which is why he built a racetrack in the deserted mountain landscape on Japan's South Island - a racetrack more splendid than any we have seen before. He calls it Autopolis, and it is here that he hangs those famous pictures of his. The candle for Pierrette flickers in a pleasant room, completely unguarded, above the medium-fast S as it sweeps into a slow right-hander.

There is a hotel in Autopolis, too, constructed to look like a galactic finish-

ing line tower. It only offers 30 rooms, and a night will set you back 700 dollars. It must be a world record-breaker when it comes to cost-to-performance ratio, especially if you stipulate a room with a view. Below you, the right-hand corner after the starting and finishing line, past that the entire track with its appealing sweeps and curves, its ups and downs, in the center a pond, on the right the stands, and behind them an arena like the Motodrom at Hockenheim. It is here, along the building's longitudinal axis, that Pierrette resides. Far away into the background a chain of volcanoes, one capped by a wisp of hovering soot. But quite apart from the view, I have never experienced a modern hotel with such an appealing sense of style about it – even if the thing about the bathrooms is somewhat over the top.

The giant panorama windows in all the rooms, which are all de facto suites, can be electronically switched from transparent to obscure at the flick of a remote control switch. Closest of all to the action are the bathrooms, everything in glass, all wonderfully transparent as long as you want it that way. At any rate you can follow the progress of the race from the tub, the cars flinging themselves into the left-hand corner while you scrub, say, your left knee. This is a phenomenon noticeable on an increasing scale everywhere you go: The desire to experience the universe from the bathtub. The most intimate of environments as a watery amplifier for the senses.

Before we lose ourselves in wondering about the motives of the bathtub racing fan, perhaps it is as well to turn our attention to the track.

It is 4.7 km long, offers plenty of variety, is easily surveyed and as safe as a racetrack can ever be. The pilots love it. Its electronic controls, monitoring and transmission are almost oppressive. You could practically take Autopolis as a whole, feed it to a satellite and direct the TV broadcast from somewhere in Europe – say from a bathtub in France.

"The toilet fittings are made of chromium steel – the ones used out on the track too", announced Peter Sauber straight away on the first day. The Swiss are known for an eye to solid quality, even behind the scenes.

As far as the racing was concerned, before the final heat it seemed that Jaguar had the World Championship easily within its grasp, although things for Peugeot were also looking up with two recent double victories. Toyota was putting in a maiden appearance with an interesting new design (V10, 5-cylinder) and Mercedes was scraping along rock bottom: Not a single victory to their name this year, not even a whiff of the finishing line for the past three races, continuous worry with the new twelve-cylinder, simply the doldrums. Ugghh.

Logically enough, the Mercedes (Schlesser/Mass and Schumacher/Wendlinger) were unable to sight land at all in the Autopolis train-ing session. Five engines gave up the ghost in quick succession, leaving only minimal time for actual driving. The culprit was still the mid-season casting batch, and it had affected 30 engines. Thirty 12-cylinders of the up-and-under league, just imagine. One of the engines might just run a reasonable distance with a little luck, extremely accurate gauging work and "by getting exactly the right bits together". The helplessness of wit-nessing this highbrow 12-cylinder project forced to resort to the most basic of improvisation tactics!

A new light emanating from the attractive but slightly indistinct background of the open valley brings out the contours with greater clarity:

The shading effects deepen on the hills, the forests appear more forceful, dark cypresses stand out like fresh strokes of a brush. Distant mountain ranges are carved out against the opening of the valley, and an honest-to-goodness volcano emerges from the clouds, complete with smoke column, as contented as a smoking chimney. Ah, I can hear you say, the exotic beauty of Kyushu, with Mount Aso advertising cigarillos.

But the day of the race began with a message from Okinawa: A typhoon by the name of Clara, designated number 23, is sweeping its way across the south, and fraying nerves throughout the region. Fog (or perhaps it was low-lying cloud) hanging over Autopolis. Too bad about the race, was on the tip of every tongue - but it remained showery and changeable, and we had learned to be patient.

Suddenly the fog cleared, and during the warm-up, cries of "Oh, look at Wendlinger" were heard on all sides.

He was right at the front, and although no-one was in any doubt that he would never see the finishing line (what other result could they expect this season?), at least the team was showing its teeth.

In the race, Schumacher took the first shift, and was an absolute smash hit. The way he tackled the Peugeots and the Jaguars, his clever, persistent harassment and the matter-of-fact way he took the lead gave us all the feeling we were dealing with a born champion here.

The fact that Mercedes was still in the lead when Wendlinger took his turn was a consolation for the Mercedes contingent. A token success at least in the last race, they would say: Up until we dropped out we were actually leading.

A Toyota spread itself incredibly wide in front of Wendlinger, who refused to be drawn to overtake, preferring to lose a few seconds. And the Mercedes was still going, the mood in the pit was ecstatic.

Behind, Warwick and Fabi were fighting it out (both Jaguar pilots were contesting for the Drivers' World Championship title), followed by Baldi in the Peugeot and Schlesser/Mass in the Senior Mercedes.

When Wendlinger was relieved by Schumacher again, they were still out in front, and Schumacher kept up the pressure.

It was as if a vision whispered months before - softly but with force and imagination - were slowly falling into place piece by piece. And today, for the first time, the vision and the reality are one: The "Juniors", this famous invention by Jochen Neerpasch, positively managed to go the whole way, turning budding talents of 19 into race winners at 22. In the best soap-opera family tradition: The respectful, obedient young learning from their elders, and now here they are driving a lap of honor in front of Jean-Louis Schlesser, World Champion in 1989 and 1990, and Jochen Mass, the most successful pilot of the entire Group C era. And at the finishing line, they will thank the old boys for their support and for tuning the cars.

For all the world like one of the great, experienced hands of the racing scene, Michael Schumacher holds the snarling, snapping Jaguars at bay right through the last laps, taking Mercedes to victory in the closing race of an era. One of the many in tears at the finishing line is Jochen Mass, who came fifth. He was a true friend to the young victor, and like Neerpasch had always held fast to the "Junior" idea. He was 44, just exactly as old as Wendlinger and Schumacher put together. Now is the time, he sobbed joyfully, for me to give up.

LIMOUSINE IN SPRINTING SHOES

OVER THE DECADES it has been the standard procedure for motor racing departments in most companies to belong to the research and development side of things. The development technicians put forward their ideas, checked out their feasibility, constructed, tested, and finally wheeled out their creations onto the racetrack. Ideally, a group would be rehoused away from the inflexibility of the parent company in their own building somewhere on the other side of town, but always structured so as to ensure a clearly running thread of responsibility by the technicians. This was especially true at Mercedes. The whole Silver Arrow concept was only conceivable removed from the mainstream of technical management, and the rallye team set up in the late seventies was organized as a matter of course in the form of an offshoot of the main testing department.

Nowadays things have shifted into a more complex gear, with the factor communication assuming a focal role. Racing cars have long since ceased to be technical weapons – they are bringers of messages.

In search of new impetus in the putting across of those messages, the motor racing division at Mercedes underwent a radical rethink at the beginning of the nineties and was regrouped in the form of a staff department. In 1994 things began to really take off the ground with the appearance of an ideal new candidate: The C-Class.

The logical platform to put across this promising new message was the German Touring Car Championship, the DTM, which commands a broad international following.

The synchronized timing between the new limousine and the racing model, between its appearance and its rise to fame, meant that the message was one that could be swallowed whole without any of the usual flavoring additives: The C-Class - a great car, a winner, technically out front, good looking. And the Mercedes people - ordinary folk, not the usual self-important types (perhaps even likable?), bringing motor racing closer to the fans, identification, participation, none of the usual steamroller tactics, and they can even lose gracefully (although there was no detailed planning carried out in this direction).

Much of the guiding spirit for the project was radiated by Norbert Haug, who possesses the rare ability to combine the go-getter with the man of sentiment in a way which is entirely natural and makes credible the claim: We are creating a car that we love, we want to give it the best we can (for best, read: highest speed for this particular segment of the company). To achieve all this at a time where scrimping and saving are the order of the day is a skill unto itself: The motor racing sector must emerge from the slimming and slicing process as lean as the new style of series production. In this particular instance, it has done just that, lending the project a whole new credibility when it comes to internal justification. Which is an important thing in view of the faction from within the company who envisage the future of Mercedes-Benz to be just as rosy

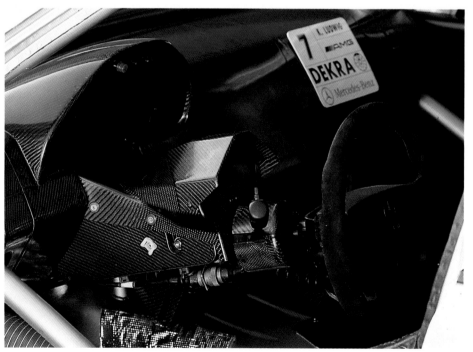

Form follows close on the heels of function. The front end is one of the car's most complex zones, this is where drag coefficient and negative lift come together, where the delicate question of the radiator zone is decided, the cooling air routing, the crash properties, fast and easy servicing, the aesthetic demands on what should be a C-Class nose

with or without motor racing involvement.

One of the main pillars of the project was the transformation of the C-Class into a racing car without destroying its identity. There is no shortage of examples from the racing world of cars which have been manipulated out of all recognition for the race-track - Mercedes itself is no stranger to them.

And indeed, the Mercedes DTM automobile is a C-Class from top to toe, a limousine in sprinting shoes.

One of the fundamental question marks hanging over the project was whether to stand ground with the classical Mercedes drive concept against the impressive stream of four-wheel drive technology overwhelming the touring car racing scene. That four-wheel drive represents the better solution under certain circumstances, but not the overwhelming majority of circumstances, is something nobody will deny. But to bring those benefits to bear here, in the extreme environment of this technically sophisticated championship which would seem to offer practically no scope for further improvement, is a different question altogether. Mercedes opted, at any rate, to back the simpler and more consistent rear-wheel drive solution – a decision which formed the focal point for the car's technical concept: To use the available depth and length for consistent weight distribution, to position the engine as far back and low down as possible, to place the transmission as centrally as the regulations permit.

The decision to side-step the additional trouble and expense was to lead in the final reckoning to a car which was more lightweight and more nifty, and ASR proved to be a sensational flanking measure to cope with emergency situations. The use of ASR in fact does much to sharpen the sensitivity of the pilot in a roundabout sort of way: The system attempts to act a step ahead of the human capacity to react, which racing drivers find a slight irritant to their natural pride. They use every trick in the book to prevent the system actually ever being used, and so in their subconscious the very presence of the system helps improve their own ability to respond.

This brand new, as yet totally unclothed series car presented the ideal starting point to hark back to one of the old virtues of classical sports car construction: Call it love of detail, call it a by-product of speed and sophisticated engineering - in those days the art of finishing off had developed into a craft unto itself, that a beautiful car would emerge from the process was a matter of course. It was beautiful as a whole and beautiful in every detail, and its very beauty lent it a personality which was beyond the mere clocking up of tenths of seconds here or there. In keeping with this tradition, special care was taken in the racing version C-Class to ensure that every solution, every feature looks the part.

Enzo Ferrari, who, thanks to his ingenious designer friends sent some of the most beautiful racing cars of all time out onto the tarmac, is reported to have said: "The most beautiful car is always the one that wins."

Seen from this perspective, the 1994 C-Class racing car is beautiful twice over.

HAPPY END

The King had seven sons and daughters...

**The classical photo of
Mercedes Jellinek-Mercedes,
which was taken 1904 in Nice**

It is one of those stories which starts out rosy and then takes an abrupt plunge. After all, fairy tales have always been about paradise lost in some form or another. In this instance the tale is interwoven by another storyline, a second dimension which allows you to reach into the book and take the hand of the only remaining survivor - a hand which is still very much alive. You can sit with her, listen to her silvery tones, her fine intonation charged with self-directed irony and all the ease which a venerable elderly lady can muster. The sister of Mercedes is now living the Happy Ending.

Although contemporary opinions diverge slightly about the historical role played by Emil Jellinek, let us agree to adopt a happy medium:

This was a man sent on his way in life with more than his fair share of personality, humor, imagination and financial means. Added to all these innate attributes, Emil Jellinek also possessed the courage to turn the passion which powered all his thoughts and actions into practical achievements. It was this talent which marked him not only as a great pioneer but primarily as the first marketing genius of the new automotive age. (To avoid being enmeshed in sophistic argument, the term genius here implies an element of fallibility).

His most important contribution towards the creation of the Mercedes legend has become a legendary act in itself: He urged Maybach and Daimler to build a more powerful engine for the Daimler-Phönix car, drove the new version to victory as "Monsieur Mercédès" in a touring event in Nice, introduced new improvements at the Cannstatt production workshops. He provided financial security by becoming a large-scale customer himself, named the car Mercedes in 1900, and went on to achieve a decisive breakthrough in 1901 at the Nice Race Week in terms of both

sporting achievement and image. From 1902, the name Mercedes was officially protected for the Daimler Motor Company.

Mercedes was the name of his then only daughter, who was born in 1889 in Vienna. There were also two older boys, Adolphe and Fernand, at the time. In 1893, Jellinek's wife died.

In 1899, Jellinek married again. His second wife was French, and presented him with three sons in quick succession, Didier (1900), Guy (1902) and René (1903).

On August 2, 1906 in Vienna, Emil Jellinek's seventh and last child was born. By this time, the family had changed its name by deed-pole to Jellinek-Mercedes, and the name was to be handed down to the coming generations. The latecomer was christened Andrée. Needless to say, just Andrée would have been out of the question in this particular family. This is where our other story begins...

N ow, as this story is narrated, Andrée Jellinek-Mercedes has turned 88 years of age, a lady of no uncertain charm and with a friendly air of determination. There is no sign of senility to be glimpsed here, either physically or mentally, only a well-developed sense of humor and intellect. The years seem to melt away as we talk in the heart of old Vienna, only two hundred yards from the St. Stephan's Cathedral.

"My father unleashed his imagination when it came to naming his children. All of us, boys as well as girls, were given a whole string of appendages - preferably Spanish. "Maria de las Mercedes" (Maria of the Merciful) was up with the favorites, and fell to my sister as her first name: Mercedes Adrienne Manuela Ramona. Papa plumped for Carmen in my case (I was perverse enough to turn out blonde and befreckled), but my mother drew the line at any more Spanish names, so I ended up with Andrée Yvonne Odette. She

gave way on the fourth name, presumably in the interests of a quiet life, and so it was decided to round me off with Maya."

Slightly germanized to become "Maja", the last name of the last Jellinek offspring was used to christen another vehicle: In 1907, the Maja-Wagen, the brainchild of Ferdinand Porsche, came onto the market. The new car originated from the Jellinek-controlled ´Österreichische Daimler-Motoren-Gesellschaft´ in Wiener Neustadt. Especially to market the Maja, a new company, the ´Österreichische Automobil-Gesellschaft (ÖAG)´ was founded. A 1907 issue of the journal ´Allgemeine Automobil Zeitung´ included a report on the Maja: "This car is a new feature of the first order. Its designer, Mr. Ferdinand Porsche, aims to show the automobile world that he is not only an expert in electrical vehicles, but also understands the intricacies of the petrol engine. While the Maja car bears many of the features of its half-sister the Mercedes, this model demonstrates a range of unique design details which merit particular acclaim."

There was also talk of the "astounding talents of the man who succeeded in launching the Mercedes car with such a degree of skill", and speculation that the success of the Mercedes would be transferred to the Maja - an assumption we now know to be completely unfounded. One of the more innovative details of the car, a new type of gearshift, had to be abandoned for a more conventional solution. Added to this, the first automobile boom was just entering its first slump. The Maja became a decided flop. In 1908, Jellinek sold all his property in Wiener Neustadt, and a short time later also terminated his participation in Daimler in Untertürkheim, Stuttgart. Ferdinand Porsche, however, was standing on the threshold of one of the most profitable and successful periods of his career with the now "Austro Daimler". The following seventeen years were the longest he was ever to stay with any one firm.

Ninety years on in Vienna's famous Prater Park: Mercedes' "little sister", Andrée Jellinek-Mercedes, with her great-granddaughter

Meine Eltern lebten in Nizza, an der Riviera. Wenn ich an meine Kindheit zurückdenke, sehe ich Sonne, das blaue Meer.

Andrée "Maya" Jellinek-Mercedes was happily oblivious of the car which bore her name. Its brief period of fame was over before she had grown out of babyhood, and the episode had long been blown over by the winds of oblivion by the time she was old enough to understand. Her sister, naturally enough, was confronted at every turn with "her" particular marque, without it meaning that much to her. No myth grew up linking her fate to that of the car - perhaps partly because of the bitterness with which her father looked back on his dealings with the Mercedes. He always considered himself to have been bought out too cheaply - despite his professed skills as a financial wizard.

" *In our family, the boys were all born as Frenchmen, the daughters as Austrians. There was logic behind this in my case: I was born in August, which meant we had taken up residence in our summer ´quarters´ in Baden near Vienna. But still, for me the dominating childhood memories revolve around Nice, our beautiful villa on the Promenade des Anglais, and romping with my brothers and sisters. My nanny was called Pepi and came from Moravia. She had been a fixture of our family for forty years, and even Papa held her in the greatest respect. I spoke German to her and to my father, while French was the language of communication with my mother and the governess.*

"I especially loved our seasonal change of residence between France and Austria. Once, Henri Rothschild lent us a saloon car to travel in. After that, Papa rented a whole sleeping car every year which was coupled to the train in Nice. Of course there was such a lot of staff to consider: The lady's maid, the tutor, the governess, the manservant. We always had the same ticket collector, whom we children became very fond of. I remember for certain that Mercedes, who had married the Viennese Baron Schlosser, came to the Villa in Baden when I was only three. For the whole family, I was the ´little one´, the little sister, an unexpected new addition, a surprise. This was reflected in the special kindness and affection Mercedes always showed me.

"My father talked himself into believing that as the ´little one´, I should be shielded from the more unpleasant aspects of life. That is why I was never allowed to go to school, where I might have caught wind of the fact that life was not all sunshine and roses."

"I was not even told when my brother died (of appendicitis). He was only eight, I was not yet five. René has gone away, was what I was told, and in my childish imagination, all I could imagine by that was that he was living in our huge and mysterious attic. One day I asked by big sister Mercedes to go up there with me to visit René...

"The Villa in Baden was a paradise on earth, too. It had 42 rooms and 25 bathrooms. The middle section, where my sister and her husband lived, was called ´Villa Mercedes´. Everything was Art Nouveau, each room had its own name – one was called the ´Kaiserzimmer´, or Emperor's room, and was decked out all in black with yellow trim. My father had an idea in his head that everyone should have their own toilet. There was a toilet behind every concealed door. Everywhere you went there were toilets... We were certainly a family with a difference.

"Mercedes was a woman with style. Her wedding in Nice was hailed as a grand occasion, despite the fact that her bridegroom was only an unimportant state official from Austria. Her dowry alone was enough to cause a sensation: A million gold crowns, as well as twelve dozen of everything to make up her trousseau.

"Mercedes would have fitted better into the present time, she would certainly have made something of herself. Her upbringing had been strict, as the upbringing for young ladies always was in those days. She was never allowed to go out alone until her marriage had been arranged. She would have liked to live a different sort of life to her public official husband. She would have liked to be an actress, she had a good voice, was amusing, and loved the company of amusing and unusual people. Our father also had something of the comedian in his blood - loved to imitate, copied accents, and had a sharp wit. Actually that applied to the whole family. He was much loved as a host, not just because of his generosity and his wealth. He dreamt up occasions like a ´dinner for seven bishops´. The Czar of Bulgaria was one of his closest friends."

"Father's business interests were so diverse that he seemed to have a finger in just about every pie. After he left Daimler, the car industry receded to insignificance for him. He naturally continued to drive a Mercedes, always red. Cars for him should only ever be red, a particular type of cherry red which was simply Mercedes red for us. In 1914 he toyed with the idea of a return to the car trade, this time with Rolls-Royce. He was the first person ever to be supplied with a colored Rolls-Royce after a long period of wrangling with the incredulous producers. I remember my brothers calling me to the yard: Come and look at Papa's new quiet car. I can still see it before me now, and how we all stood round the quiet car with a sort of reverence. It was the red Rolls-Royce. Then came the summer when Papa went to Kissingen to take the waters. For some reason or another, we were to go into the mountains that year. We were staying in the Südbahnhotel in Semmering when war broke out. We drove home to the Villa in Baden."

1910, the Kurpark in Baden near Vienna: Baron Schlosser with his wife, 21-year-old Mercedes, and her sister Andrée

Everything which had contributed towards the liberality of the Jellinek-Mercedes family as it traveled between countries and across borders as a matter of course, turned against them in the throes of war. All their possessions in France were confiscated, while in Austria the French connections of the family had to be kept concealed. The liberal imagination of Jellinek himself unbridled the embittered imaginations of evil-wishers and of the envious: Someone like him, based in neutral Switzerland, must be the obvious choice for a spy. Emil Jellinek first returned by rail to Baden to hold together and reposition his family. The war was sure to be over soon. Meran was the best substitute for the Riviera over the winter.

The old lady reminisces: "Father said the war was bound to be finished before long, and that in Switzerland we would be closer to France. Mama would be allowed to speak French and have French contacts. So we moved to the Hotel National in Geneva, still with the customary ten to twelve rooms which our entourage required. Here, the world as we knew it was still intact: The Hotel had its own dining room for the guests' staff, the most expensive floor was the first floor, which was occupied by the super-rich from Russia.

"But the war simply did not stop. I can remember now how guests moved from one suite to the next, chamber maids carrying suitcases, somebody moving up to the next floor. Soon we were moving up too. Then the campaigns insinuating that my father was a German spy got under way in earnest. This was probably what sparked off the stroke which led to his death. As usual, we children were shielded from what was going on."

Emil Jellinek-Mercedes died on January 21, 1918, in Geneva at the age of 64.

Big sister Mercedes was safe in Austria as Frau Schlosser, mother

The original: General Consul Emil Jellinek

of two children. For the "little one" and her mother, there followed a nomadic existence which took them finally - with a Hungarian Laissez-Passer and the hope of gaining Czechoslovakian nationality (on the strength of the family's roots in Moravia!) - to Paris. "The best thing about it for me was that I was finally allowed to go to school for the first time, at the age of thirteen to fifteen! I loved it."

Slowly, things began to normalize again. The family was now, once again, for the large part French, although not allowed to use the appendage Mercedes or even Mercédès. The "little one" was a Czechoslovakian citizen. The family regained the majority of its possessions, including the Villa in Nice.

Somehow, the "little one" felt herself strangely isolated in France, and was unable to really comprehend her mother's devastation;

Madame continued to wear black. She must have loved her husband very much. At any rate Andrée was frequently sent to stay with her sister in Vienna and was swept off her feet by the "kiss-your-hand" reception still afforded to the unmarried daughters of good family in this part of the world as it had been in the days of the Kaiser. She fell in love at 18, and was quickly married. She was undoubtedly a good match. Her lord liege was only insignificantly older, tall, chic, romantic, easily enthused, and was not adverse to combining his enthusiasm for his bride with a way of reviving the flagging fortunes of his Viennese business concern.

The two sisters now lived in close proximity to each other. For the elder sister Mercedes, "born into the wrong time", the swinging twenties brought an opportunity to find her true self. At least to look for her true self. She left husband and children to marry a sculptor with a bohemian way of life, who also happened to be a Baron: Rudolf Weigl. He was consumptive, that much she knew. What she did not know was that he was an epileptic. He never made a name as an artist.

The younger sister: "I think it was an ever-present longing for the artistic life which left her no peace. She was prepared to sacrifice everything to pursue that dream; to abandon home and hearth, her reputation, even her children."

The dream went drastically wrong, and when Mercedes could no longer live the lie, she went through a second divorce. The sculptor died soon afterwards. Rejected by "society", she continued to live in artistic circles with the support of her younger sister and her husband. The fact that the automobile marque which bore her name had since gained lasting international acclaim was something which touched her not in the slightest. She had never possessed a car.

Andrée Jellinek-Mercedes: "At the end of the twenties, we all rea-

lized she must have some serious illness, probably bone cancer. She had become emaciated, and was in pain. When we went to visit her on the occasion which would turn out to be the last, we asked what she would like us to bring. She asked for a bottle of champagne."

Mercedes died on February 23, 1929, in Vienna. She had reached the age of 39.

Mercedes is buried in Vienna's central cemetery, and even less care than is generally customary in Vienna was taken over the details: The date of birth is out by ten years (1899 instead of 1889), and she is named Mercedes Schlosser Jellinek-Mercedes after her first marriage rather than her second one. This reflects the abhorrence felt by all the Jellinek family for Weigl, and was ordered by her brother Fernand. Fernand was later to commit suicide in desperation under the Nazi regime and today lies in the same spot. The gravestone is weathered, but occasional claims of "neglect" are an exaggeration: A naturally weathered grave carries something of dignity about it, and the mourning figure of a woman which has watched over the site since the death of the eldest brother Aldolphe in 1904 is one of the most attractive ways to grace any place of rest.

Between the wars, Andrée Jellinek-Mercedes lived in Vienna, where she gave birth to a daughter. She led a "wonderful, fun-filled life with a somewhat reckless husband who was certainly amusing. We were never bored." They twice took part together in the Rallye Monte Carlo in a Steyr XII (starting in Königsberg, now Kaliningrad!), and even planned a trip through the Sahara. To get himself used to desert conditions, her husband took his lunch in the heat of summer wearing a hat and coat in the beautiful Viennese district of Hietzing. He also cherished am-

bitions of going into the movies: "He was such an interesting man, we did an awful lot together." This interesting man founded a militia in pre-Anschluss Austria, a "corps" supporting the cause of Austrian Chancellor Schuschnigg in his bid to ward off the impending Nazi takeover. This made him something of a personality in the Austria of those days, and placed him directly in the line of fire on March 12th and 13th, 1938, the date of Hitler's triumphant entry into Vienna. He was one of the first to be taken away by the new Nazi regime.

Andrée Jellinek-Mercedes was considered a "half-breed of the first order". Definite documentary proof which might have offered an escape from Nazi persecution was provided by an old confidant of her father's, a Daimler-Benz man, only shortly before the end of the war: That she was, in reality, a "100% Arian", and that the conversion to Judaism had only happened somewhere down the line of Jellinek generations.

Her husband's family turned out to be efficient in the Nazi cause and true antisemitists. Her daughter was defamed as the child of a Schuschnigg follower, her husband interned. Andrée was forced to endure all the stages of degradation and indignity at the hands of the Nazis; brownshirts in her apartment, confiscation of her possessions. Her husband was transferred to the concentration camp at Dachau. Released halfway through the war, he divorced the "half-breed of the first order". She was forced to work in factories until she was discharged on medical grounds as she began to suffer from deafness and impaired vision, and was unable to stand up straight. Her mother had since died in Paris, had "practically starved to death", with none of her children able to get through to help her.

The post-war period in the Russian zone of occupation. The Villa, this incredible edifice in Baden with all its Art Nouveau

treasures, blew up in its entirety one night. The force of the blast led to speculation that the Russians had been dancing on a former Nazi ammunitions depot. Officially, the building had been requisitioned by the Red Cross during the war.

All that was left was the gardener's lodge, a building which would today be taken for a splendid villa in itself. An inquiry in a local paper whether anyone was still alive who knew the Villa when it was still standing led to a single line of enquiry: The "little sister" was still alive. She was still living in Vienna, where her daughter had married the Austrian diplomat Dr. Ludwig Steiner. She has grandchildren and great grandchildren.

The Director of the Mercedes-Benz Museum, Max von Pein, made contact with her, and a commemorative plaque was unveiled with much ado in Baden. After this occasion, the "little sister" went missing once again, until news of the death of Andrée Jellinek-Mercedes came from Paris. This turned out to concern not the "little sister", but the second wife of her Brother Didier, who also happened to be called Andrée. Letters came written in the unmistakable purple ink which the "little sister" had used without changing for the last three-quarters of a century: "I am still alive."

Vienna, June 1994

The photographer and the authors would like to offer a personal vote of thanks to all those people and institutions whose special kindness and competence helped make an otherwise lonely project into a product of successful team work:

Special thanks to Mercedes-Benz AG also

Nancy Aronson • Luis Barragán, Balcarce • Béla Barénji • B. Braun-Melsungen AG • Uwe Brodbeck • Le Chateau de Versailles • Cerruti 1881, Paris • Le Conservatoire de la Plaisance de Bordeaux
Elektrizitätsversorgung Schwaben, Heilbronn • Juan Manuel Fangio and friends • Frankfurt Airport and Deutsche Lufthansa • Les Feutres Ultramod, Paris • Andrée Jellinek-Mercedes and her great-granddaughter • Denis Jenkinson
Peterheinz Kern • Karl Kling • Kosaïdo Golfclub, Düsseldorf • Kunstmuseum, Bonn • Wilf Lamers • Ralph Lauren • Jan Melin • Stirling Moss • Dr. Harry Niemann • O. Noda • R. Nomura • R. Ogawa • Max-Gerrit von Pein
Stanislav Peschel • Edzard Reuter • Dieter Ritter • Wolfgang Rolli • Peter Sauber • Herbert Völker

LITERATURE

Archiv Mercedes-Benz AG, Museum, Stuttgart • Adriano Cimarosti: Autorennen, Hallwag, Berne, 1986 • Juan Manuel Fangio/Roberto Carozzo: Fangio: My racing life, Patrick Stephens Ltd., Wellingborough, 1990
Guy Jellinek-Mercédès: Mein Vater der Herr Mercedes, Paul Neff, Vienna, 1962 • Denis Jenkinson: With Moss in the Mille Miglia, Motor Sport, Tee & Whiten and J. Mead Ltd., London, 1955 • Shotaro Kobayashi,
Emperor's Mercedes, Auto Topics, Los Angeles, 1963 • Jakob Lehmann/Harry Niemann: Hans Liska - Lächeln, Lorbeer, Leidenschaften, Motorbuch Verlag, Stuttgart, 1993 • Karl Ludvigsen: The Mercedes-Benz Racing Cars,
Bond/Parkhurst Books, London, 1971 • Jan Melin: Mercedes-Benz. The supercharged 8-cylinder cars of the 1930s, Nordbok International Co-editions AG, Gothernburg, 1985 • Jan Melin: Mercedes-Benz 8 cylindrar,
1930-talets kompressorvagnar i Norden, Bienen & Haventon AB, Höör, 1992 • Günther Molter: Juan Manuel Fangio und seine Gegner, Motorbuch Verlag, Stuttgart, 1967 • George Monkhouse: Mercedes-Benz Grand Prix Racing
1934 - 1939, White Mouse Editions, London, 1983 • Stirling Moss/Doug Nye: Fangio, Ein Pirelli-Album, Heel, Königswinter, 1991 • Alfred Neubauer/Harvey T. Rowe: Männer, Frauen und Motoren, Motorbuch Verlag, Stuttgart,
1970 • Werner Oswald: Mercedes-Benz Personenwagen 1886 - 1986, Motorbuch Verlag, Stuttgart, 1986 • Halwart Schrader: Mercedes-Benz Silberpfeile, BLV Verlagsgesellschaft, Munich/Vienna, 1987 • Halwart Schrader/
Carlo Demand: Mercedes Kompressorwagen, Edita, Lausanne, Schrader & Partner, Munich, 1979 • Paul Simsa/Jürgen Lewandowski: Sterne, Stars und Majestäten, Stadler, Constance, 1985 • Werner Walz: Daimler-Benz,
Wo das Auto anfing, Stadler, Constance, 1989

PHOTO CREDITS

All colour photos: Peter Vann
Black and white photos: Mercedes-Benz AG Archive, Heikki Jaakola, Nils Johansson, Louis Klemantaski (The Klemantaski Collection, Stanford)